HENRY V's BROTHER

HENRY V'S BROTHER

JOHN OF LANCASTER, REGENT OF FRANCE

JOANNA ARMAN

PEN & SWORD HISTORY

AN IMPRINT OF PEN & SWORD BOOKS LTD.
YORKSHIRE – PHILADELPHIA

First published in Great Britain in 2025 by
PEN AND SWORD HISTORY
An imprint of
Pen & Sword Books Ltd
Yorkshire – Philadelphia

Copyright © Joanna Arman, 2025

ISBN 978 1 39900 446 6

Typeset in Times New Roman 12/16 by
SJmagic DESIGN SERVICES, India.
Printed and bound in the UK by CPI Group (UK) Ltd.

The Publisher's authorised representative in the EU for product safety is
Authorised Rep Compliance Ltd., Ground Floor, 71 Lower Baggot Street,
Dublin D02 P593, Ireland.
www.arccompliance.com

For a complete list of Pen & Sword titles please contact:
PEN & SWORD BOOKS LIMITED
George House, Units 12 & 13, Beevor Street, Off Pontefract Road,
Barnsley, South Yorkshire, S71 1HN, England
E-mail: enquiries@pen-and-sword.co.uk
Website: www.pen-and-sword.co.uk

or

PEN AND SWORD BOOKS
1950 Lawrence Rd, Havertown, PA 19083, USA
E-mail: uspen-and-sword@casematepublishers.com
Website: www.penandswordbooks.com

Contents

Preface

For this, my fourth book, I am returning once again to the fifteenth century where I spent so much time during my days as a postgrad student but with one difference. All three of my other biographies have been of medieval royal women: this is my first book about a man. Also, for the first time, my subject was not a ruler or a monarch, at least not officially.

John of Lancaster, Duke of Bedford (1389–1435) was the son, brother, and uncle of three successive monarchs. He did not rise to prominence until he was in his thirties, late by medieval standards, and did not even attain the rank of duke until he was 24 years of age. For most of his life, John remained in the background of history. As a younger son, he was not the heir to his father or to his brother (except for a few months in 1421), but unlike some younger sons from history, John never sought power or preference for himself. His career from his youth was marked by loyal and dedicated service to his family. First as Warden of the East March, in which he patrolled the northern border of England, protected it from its enemies, and later as the Lieutenant of England.

Even though he was the second youngest of Henry V's brothers, he was the one Henry trusted the most ahead of his older brother the Duke of Clarence. He was placed in charge of England in the absence of his warlike brother, Henry V. In fact, he was the de facto ruler of England for half of his brother's reign. Upon his death, John took on the mantle of regent of France: the protector and defender of the English territories there until his nephew Henry VI could be crowned king.

In an age when Englishmen were treated with suspicion and hostility by most people in France Bedford stood out as an exception. Even his enemies spoke well of him for his sense of justice, honour and desire to protect the people and land entrusted to his care. Although he was not the famous military leader that Henry V would become, John, Duke of Bedford, led England to victory at the Battle of Verneuil in 1424. The battle is largely forgotten today but is being reconsidered by some historians who argue that it was at least as important and decisive as Agincourt. Indeed, it has been dubbed the 'Second Agincourt' because of its importance and the scale of the victory against the odds.

John, like his siblings, was an educated man who had a great fondness for books and the arts. On his marriage to Anne, sister of the duke of Burgundy, in 1423, he presented his wife with the gift of a beautiful, illuminated book of hours: a type of prayer book. The book survives today because Anne gifted it to her nephew Henry VI of England a few years later. Today, it is housed in the British Library. This rare treasure of a book contains several portraits of John and his wife, Anne as well as their coats of arms. From it, we know that John bore a great resemblance to his father Henry IV and his brother Henry V.

As with so many historical figures, however, there was to be no happy ending for John. His decades-long career as the guardian of his family's legacy ultimately ended in failure. His greatest ally, the Duke of Burgundy, defected to the French side, despite the best efforts of Bedford to preserve their alliance. Bedford died, distraught, only a few days before Burgundy was formally reconciled with his enemies with the Treaty of Arras. He was only 46 years old. Bedford also never managed to produce a single legitimate child, despite being married for ten years to Anne and marrying again after her death. It was this failure, perhaps, which caused John the most personal distress.

In the modern world, Bedford is generally only known as the villain in movies about Joan of Arc and is often seen (unfairly) as the architect of her fate. The last year of his life was marked with failure, and because the English ultimately lost almost all of the territory in France which his brother fought to obtain, this legacy of failure is usually also projected onto Bedford. This is, I believe an unfair assessment. For most of his life, and indeed most of his career, Bedford was a gifted and respected leader both in England and in France. He was overshadowed by his brother purely because of the order of his birth: but also because of his personal qualities. For more than a decade after his brother's death, he managed to protect, defend and maintain the English kingdom of France: an entity which had not existed since the century after the Norman Conquest. No one but the duke of Bedford was ever able to persuade Henry VI to return to France.

Had Bedford lived longer, and if he'd had a legitimate son, it isn't unreasonable to suggest that the path of history may have run differently. He might not have been able to prevent the Anglo-Burgundian alliance from breaking down, but he could have continued his effective defence of English possessions there and opposed the damaging foreign policy of the 1440s. What's more, a child of the beloved duke of Bedford could have bolstered the reputation and popularity of the House of Lancaster during the troubled years of Henry VI's reign. He could even have presented a viable alternative heir and successor to Henry.

He had at least two illegitimate children by an unknown woman or women. His bastard son, Richard, was apparently legitimised by Henry VI only a year or so after his father's death, but he was not able to succeed to any of Bedford's lands or titles and apparently died before Henry's reign descended into chaos. His illegitimate daughter named Mary was swept along by the fortunes of the war in France. Married to a petty French lord for many years, she was eventually forced to return to England when her husband was executed because he fought for the English against the king of France and died in obscurity. Her children remained in France and had little connection to their mother's or grandfather's homeland. Did they even know that their grandfather had been the brother of Henry V and the regent of France? If they did, it was something they kept very quiet about.

John was buried in Rouen Cathedral: he had spent much of the last fifteen years of his life in France and rarely returned to England during that time. Following his appointment as regent and marriage it became his real home. His grave remained there until the French Revolution when it was destroyed along with many other artefacts and buildings from the medieval period. John's grave wasn't targeted specifically because he was English or a representative of foreign conquest, but rather as part of the general iconoclasm directed against all things royal during a turbulent period in French history. As a result of this destruction, the only connection we really have to John is the splendid Bedford Hours, and the trial of evidence from various medieval records.

Only one other biography of John, Duke of Bedford exists which was written in the 1960s by Ethel Carleton Williams. Williams' study is useful and important, but at times she does make arbitrary character judgements about historical figures without much evidence or elaboration. Nevertheless, her book provided an important framework for this one. Richard Wadge's study on the Battle of Verneuil (2016) also provides us with a short, partial biography of John. Other studies on the final third of John's life, when he served as the regent of France can be found in Juliet Barker's *Conquest: The English Kingdom of France* (2010) as well as the latest volume in Johnathan Sumption's history of the Hundred Years' War, *Triumph and Illusion* (2023).

I first encountered John Duke of Bedford during my research for my dissertation more than thirteen years ago, and since then I have always been a fan of Henry V's enigmatic but often overlooked younger brother. Some historians see John as the model ruler Henry V should have been, a man who served his country and worked for the good of the people in his charge but didn't have his brother's rough edges or ruthless streak. John seems to have had the good fortune to have been a man who had all the good qualities of his brother but shared none of the controversy surrounding his actions or reputation. Since he was not a king, he was able to get away with more and make difficult choices which didn't necessarily reflect badly on him as he was technically acting on the behalf of others. Yet John was not purely a pragmatist and never seems to have been acting purely out of self-interest.

Yet it's easy to idealise John and his actions should be considered in the context of his time and the political context in which he was forced to operate. Behind the scenes, John often carried out the orders of his brother, his nephew or others: as a youth he had been involved in the arrest of the archbishop of York who was later executed. The death of Joan of Arc is often blamed on John. It is the only real stain on his reputation and one which seems impossible to wash off. In his position though, it seems unlikely that any other ruler would have dealt with the visionary French teenager in any other way. He had loyally served the interests of England and fought to uphold his brother's legacy for most of his life and could do nothing less than ensure any threat to them was removed. Neither would John have entertained anyone saying a word against his beloved brother Henry, nor his father, Henry IV. John was, in other words, thoroughly a man of his time.

Nonetheless, his abilities, his sense of fairness and his desire to ensure that the people he was entrusted to rule over as guardian of England or regent of France were treated with justice and equity ensured that John was remembered even by his adversaries as a good man. John's determination is often what held the English kingdom of France together and saved important cities and population centres: by sheer force of will as well as a measure of cunning and charisma he was able to stop Joan of Arc herself from taking Paris. He used his wife as a spy to keep an eye on her brother, the Duke of Burgundy, ensuring his loyalty at this vital time. He was able to bring other royal dukes to heel more than once, forcefully reminding them of their oaths to the English and to the treaty which had made his brother heir to the throne of France.

It was John who ensured Henry VI was crowned in England and France: and it is interesting to note that all of England's major military losses and defeats until 1435 occurred when John was not in command or physically present. When John died in 1435, English rule in France was basically doomed. Although they technically still retained Normandy for fifteen years after his death, continual rebellions, uprisings and the recapture of towns and cities throughout Normandy and other regions ate away at English authority and rule until the English were on the defensive. No commander as capable, steadfast and successful ever replaced John and none was ever able to command the support and financial backing for the war effort which he had been able to do.

The death of John, Duke of Bedford was also the last gasp of the House of Lancaster. Never again would they produce a military leader of the calibre of Henry V or a ruler as strong and well-beloved as John. Within thirty years of his death, the Lancastrians had not only lost all their possessions in France but also the throne of England. John would probably have been glad he did not live to see his nephew deposed by Edward, the son of the duke of York or his nephew's wife, Margaret of Anjou, rely time and time again on French mercenaries in her attempts to restore her husband to his rightful place on the throne of England. Yet that is another story, which has already been told.

Part One

RICHARD II
1389–1399

Chapter One

Third Son of Lancaster

Birth

On 20 June 1389 a woman named Mary gave birth to a son. Mary de Bohun is one of the forgotten women of medieval English history, even though she was the wife of one king, and the mother to another. Yet Mary is not listed among the queens of England, because her husband was not the king when they were married. In 1389, he was Henry Bolingbroke, or Henry of Lancaster, Earl of Derby, and the son she bore that year was not even their heir. Baby John already had two older siblings, Henry, the firstborn, and Thomas, born a year later. Henry would later become King Henry V of England. Henry Bolingbroke, Earl of Derby was, by turn, the eldest son and heir of John of Gaunt, Duke of Lancaster. Their firstborn son was obviously named after his father, their second after John of Gaunt's younger brother, Thomas of Woodstock. They named their third son after his grandfather and the incumbent duke, John of Gaunt himself.

Although his parents were thrilled to welcome another child, the third son of the earl was not considered important enough for the place of his birth to have been recorded. He may have been born on his father's lands on the Welsh borders. Henry was elevated to the rank of duke of Hereford by Richard II, and his firstborn and namesake son Henry was actually born in Monmouth, but John may have been born in Kenilworth. It's hard to know for certain because the family divided their time between various properties on Henry's lands, including Kenilworth, Tutbury and Hereford or Berkhamsted castles.[1]

Mary de Bohun's life is worth exploring. She was the youngest daughter of Humphrey de Bohun, and together with her sister, she was the co-heiress of the estates and titles of the once-great de Bohun family. Their father was Humphrey de Bohun, Earl of Hereford who was based at Pleshey Castle in Essex. The family had been around since the time of William the Conqueror and, at one point, had been one of the most prominent Marcher families. The Marchers were families who held land on the borders of Wales and Scotland, and were supposed to maintain law, order and royal authority in those regions. At least that was the theory: often the Marcher lords became something like petty kings in their own right.

In the fourteenth century, Pleshey Castle was a cultured and luxurious residence. Today all that is left is two large artificial mounds, one round and the other larger, crescent moon-shaped with a bridge connecting them. Pleshey was constructed in the classic motte and bailey design introduced to England by the Normans. The small, rounded mound was the site of the keep, the main defensive structure of the castle. Over the bridge which spanned the moat dividing the motte from the bailey, there was a whole complex of buildings enclosed within the curtain wall. These were thought to include a hall with adjoining buttery and pantry as well as a gatehouse, chapel and private apartments.

There was controversy about Mary's marriage to Henry, though her mother obviously approved. Earl Humphrey died at the age of 31 leaving only two underage daughters as his heirs, but he did have a male cousin, Gilbert. One who, by rights, perhaps should have inherited the family's lands. Instead, the estates were divided among his two surviving daughters, Mary and Eleanor. Eleanor was married to Thomas of Woodstock, the youngest surviving son of Edward III in 1376. Later tradition had it that her family wanted Mary to go into a nunnery so that her older sister and her heirs could keep the family inheritance intact. The medieval chronicler Froissart seemed to believe this and suggests that John of Gaunt purchased her marriage when his brother was away, and then made the marriage come about by abducting the young Mary when she visited her grandmother.

This almost certainly wasn't true and was probably a later explanation for the tension between John of Gaunt and his brother, Mary's brother-in-law, after the marriage. We do know that Mary married Henry by February 1381. He was only 14 years of age, and she was barely 11. Child marriages like theirs were not uncommon, but nor were they expected to be full marriages. Little Mary was sent to live with her mother Joan de Bohun, née Fitzalan, after the wedding and stayed with her for several years. She wasn't expected to cohabit with her husband at such an age, despite some rumours that the marriage was consummated straight away.

There is a hiatus between Mary de Bohun's marriage and the birth of her children, understandable considering she was underage when it took place and the years she spent with her mother. She returned to living with her husband again in early 1386 by which time she would have been 16 or 17 years old. A much more acceptable age for a couple to be cohabiting. Their first child was born in late August 1436 and over the next seven years, Mary gave birth to a further five children. The year after John, in 1390, Mary gave birth to her fourth and final son Humphrey. She had two more children by her husband after four sons in a row. Their first of two daughters, Blanche, was born in 1392 and their second daughter, Philippa was born in 1394.

Her time after that was taken up by maintaining her husband's household and raising her children. John and Thomas, his next older brother, had a nurse called Joanna Donnesmere. She was most likely not a wet nurse (so she didn't breastfeed the children), and instead looked after their daily needs as infants. She was paid the generous sum of 40 shillings per year for her work. When he was little more than a mere toddler, John was also provided with a 'varlet': which purely meant a man, or more likely a boy who acted as a servant or attendant.[2]

We know that Mary de Bohun enjoyed music and played an instrument which was like an early version of a guitar, loved books and liked animals. She had pet greyhounds which she doted on, and her husband once bought her a parrot he had acquired as a present in his travels around Europe returning from the Holy Land. The noise must have gone down well with the children, who likely loved to hear it sing and talk. Mary's love of music was inherited by her boys: although it may seem hard to believe, her firstborn son who became the famous warrior King Henry V was a keen musician. Henry played the harp from a young age and mastered some kind of wind instrument which may have been a flute, recorder or even some medieval form of the bagpipes.[3]

All her boys also inherited her love of literature and reading, and there is some suggestion that Henry as an adult may have written a musical score for the use in religious services. Like her oldest son's love of music, the love of literature and the written word was lifelong for all of Mary's sons, including John. Mary's father, Duke Humphrey had also commissioned a book of hours, but it was not finished at the time of his death. His wife and daughters continued the family tradition of commissioning manuscripts and the love of the written word. It wasn't just their mother who loved books and the written word though: Henry, earl of Derby could read and write in no fewer than three languages, English, French and Latin and was a 'bookworm' himself. He was also a friend of the poet Geoffrey Chaucer who had long associations with the Lancastrian family: his first book, *The Book of the Duchess*, was about Henry's mother Blanche of Lancaster, and Chaucer's wife may have been the sister of the sister of John of Gaunt's long-term mistress, Katherine Swynford.

A book of hours was listed among the possessions of Mary de Bohun, it might have been the one which was started for her father when she was a child and completed for her. Mary de Bohun's mother also commissioned a psalter, or a small book containing the psalms, to be made for her daughter to celebrate her marriage. The psalter contained several illustrations, including one showing the livery of the Bohun family quartered or combined with that of the Lancastrian family. Decades later, the wife of John, duke of Bedford would present a lavishly illustrated book to her nephew, the young King Henry VI (and Mary's grandson). That book became known as the Bedford Hours and is one of the most beautiful and remarkable survivals of a late-medieval illustrated manuscript. John followed the example of his grandmother and had the book illustrated with reminders of the person who had commissioned it, including a full-length portrait of himself and his wife.

Henry of Monmouth was by then 9 years of age: he would probably have begun his formal education under the supervision of tutors at the age of 7, or even as young as 5. Education for the children of fifteenth-century nobles was typically quite structured. In the mornings, children would take formal lessons in Latin, French perhaps a smattering of mathematics, although this was more directed towards making basic calculations. Lessons such as that began as early as 4 years of age, and reading may have begun even earlier. Later in the day, youngsters would be occupied with the more practical skills of medieval life: riding, archery, or practising on their favourite musical instruments which the Lancastrian children were almost as keen on as books. For boys, there would of course have been more emphasis on martial skills such as swordplay and jousting, whereas girls were encouraged to partake in activities such as embroidery and sewing but weren't excluded from taking up things like riding and archery since they lent themselves to hunting which was popular with both genders.[4] At some point, perhaps as a young adult rather than a teen, John learned to use a poleaxe, a weapon which became popular with nobles in the fourteenth and fifteenth centuries. The poleaxe, or battle-axe, was a long-handled weapon with an axe blade on the end of a long pole. On the other side, balancing out the axe head was a hammer-like head, and the weapon was tipped with a spike. It was basically two weapons in one. It also took great skill and practice to learn to use one effectively because the weapon was so long it was more like quarterstaff fighting. The poleaxe could also only be used on foot, which suited the type of tactics the English were later to use in France.

Most of John and his siblings' formal lessons which didn't involve martial arts would have been given under the supervision of tutors. Tutors were almost invariably men, though there were exceptions to this. Often, they were clerics or priests who might take on such work in the early part of their career before being ordained or getting their own parish or church to work in. There were some cases of tutors to noble and royal children being laymen: one notable example was Sir Simon Burley who was tutor to the young King Richard II. Before being appointed to his office by the Black Prince, he had been a distinguished soldier and a member of the prince's household. He was not chosen for his abilities as an educator but for his connection to the father of Richard II and the loyal service he had given to the family.

Henry Bolingbroke, although he was often absent from his children's lives nevertheless made ample provision for their education. In 1395, he gave his eldest son Henry 'seven books of Latin grammar'.[5] By the time he was 9, the future King Henry V was clearly studying Latin in-depth and needed several books to work from. For the younger children, the curriculum was similar if not quite as rigorous: John received a book of Latin grammar like his brother when he was 8 years of age in 1398 and his sisters, Blanche and Philippa received 'books of ABC' at the ages of 2 and 4 respectively.[6] Blanche would have been just starting her lessons by that time, and so just started to use them, but it is doubtful what use her 2-year-old sister would have made of her book. Perhaps she just enjoyed looking at it and pointing at the letters.

It is hard to tell exactly what these 'books of ABC' contained, but they were probably short booklets intended to help children learn the rudiments of the alphabet which could be made by a cleric or scribe quite cheaply and easily. They may have had some simple illustrations or illuminations or pages left blank for copying. Why didn't John have such a book at such a young age? He obviously knew the alphabet and how to read well enough by the age of 8 to start learning Latin. It's possible that there is no record of such a thing because John's mother taught him herself when he was a similar age to his sisters. It wasn't uncommon for mothers to teach their children, even noblewomen. Some left it to tutors, but not all parents did: perhaps we do not have the records. After their mother's death, John's sister certainly needed books and tutors to teach them to read and write. E. Carleton William suggested John wasn't at the same level as his brother Henry and didn't show the same 'youthful promise' which was maybe why he received only one book to study from whereas his brother had several because his brother was excelling so much (or maybe Henry passed on the books which he had finished with them). When he was young John probably had the same tutors as his sisters who taught them a variety of subjects, but when he got older, he got a personal tutor of his own. His two older brothers similarly had separate tutors: Henry's was a man named Peter Melbourne and Thomas' tutor had the rather more unusual name of Winslow Dorstayner. A man named Thomas Rothwell was picked for the young John. Boys were given personal tutors or governors when they moved onto the second stage of their education at the age of 7 or 8, which would have involved learning to use weapons, riding and hunting skills. These were of course necessary to prepare them for participation in combat and military leadership as they got older. Their tutors though ensured their academic education didn't fall by the wayside.

A knowledge of Latin was, arguably, essential for nobles in the fifteenth century. It was no longer the preserve of clerics and churchmen: by the later medieval period it was in the interests of nobles and the gentry to understand the language of law, administration and religion: of course, many secular books were written in Latin as well. Even though English would have been their first language, Henry's children would almost certainly have learned French as well. There is a charming scene in Shakespeare's *Henry V* in which the king struggles to get his tongue around some basic French phrases to impress his future bride, but it is pure fiction: the future Henry V and his siblings would have spoken French fluently. It was essential to know the language of the neighbouring country, even one with which England had a troubled and often adversarial relationship.

Henry of Bolingbroke and Mary's children came from a family of book collectors and both their parents were lovers of the written word. Humphrey, Duke of Gloucester had owned some 123 books: some of them may have come from the collection of Humphrey de Bohun, Mary's father. These books were catalogued and included not just service books, psalters and religious texts, but also the medieval version of popular fiction: romances. Thomas of Woodstock's collection included *The Romance of the Rose*, and romances about Alexander the Great, Merlin, Lancelot and Godfrey de Bouillon.[7] Under Humphrey de Bohun and his forbears, a group of Augustinian monks lived at Pleshey Castle who specialised in copying and producing manuscripts for the family. Humphrey de Bohun, like his uncle before him, was interested in books and collected them as well as having several made for himself. These are also known to have included various romances and legends, including a thirteenth-century romance known as *William and the Werewolf*. Yes, werewolf stories existed in the Middle Ages, but they were more like shapeshifters, and the story was about a young man raised by such an unfortunate creature.

The love of books which Henry and Mary encouraged in their children stayed with them for the rest of their lives. Henry of Monmouth (the future Henry V) and John were both ardent collectors of books. They even read some of them. Humphrey, the youngest son would later be known as the most learned and became famous for his love of classical and popular literature: he later named his own children Arthur, for the legendary king, and Antigone after a legendary Theban princess who features in several classical tragedies. The latter was a highly unusual naming choice for the child of a fifteenth-century aristocrat.

At some point before the end of the last decade of the fourteenth century, John went from residing primarily at Bytham Castle to Framlingham Castle in Suffolk. This latter was the residence of the elderly Margaret, duchess of Norfolk. His brother, Henry also lived there at intervals in the late 1390s allowing for a valuable period in which the two siblings may well have formed close bonds that lasted for the rest of their lives. Henry was later noted for being closer to John than any of his other siblings and entrusting him with more responsibilities.

It is interesting that he was closer to his second youngest brother than Thomas, who was only one year his junior. This might have been because Henry suffered a lot of ill health as a child and was said to have been very small and weak even as a baby: to the point that his parents feared he would not survive. He may still have been at Bytham when a physician was summoned from London to tend him because he was taken ill again in 1395. It must have been a tense time for his family and especially the children who had lost their mother only the year before. Perhaps he was even sent there to convalesce and was able to spend time with the 6-year-old John.

Young Henry may alternatively have been sent to live in a place called Courtfield Manor in Welsh Bicknor where he was placed under the care of Margaret Montagu. Lady Margaret is a fascinating figure: she was a septuagenarian by the 1390s and was a great-granddaughter of Edward I. Her paternal grandparents were King Edward's his famous daughter, Joan of Acre and her controversial second husband. She died in 1395, only a year after Henry's mother, and afterwards he was in the care of her daughter-in-law the countess of Salisbury. Her husband, John Montagu, the incumbent Earl of Salisbury, was a friend of Henry Bolingbroke, although in a twist of fate he later proved to be one of the only nobles who was unfaltering in his loyalty to Richard II. Henry may have moved around a lot and not been based with his guardians all the time, and obviously his father took him to London at least once, although after 1395 he seems to have favoured his second son to take on trips and journeys away from home with him.

For these first few years of his young life, John grew up in the care of his mother and among his ever-growing number of siblings in a household that must have been bustling and full of life, energy and (probably) domestic drama and felt the absence of his father. The year after John's birth, when Mary de Bohun was probably still pregnant with his brother Humphrey, his father attended a tournament in Calais where he won great renown. Henry Bolingbroke was still a young man in his twenties and decided that simply travelling to France for a tournament didn't quite satisfy his thirst for adventure enough. So, after only a few weeks back home he decided to go on a military expedition against the Lithuanians: Lithuania in the late fourteenth century was still (officially) a pagan state, and so it was the focus of a crusade led by the Teutonic Knights, one the last remaining crusading orders in Europe. Henry was with them for nearly a year and joined in with the siege of the city of Vilnius. The crusade against Lithuania had actually been going on for more than a century, and in 1390 it was less a religious war and more of a partisan participation in a Lithuanian dynastic dispute. The Teutonic Knights were fighting against a ruler who had helped to convert the Lithuanians: which was supposed to be the very thing which they wanted. Henry went first to Prussia and then spent several months over the autumn and winter at the siege where he was supposed to have taken 'three dukes' captive and killed hundreds of other enemy soldiers and carried off women and children back to Königsberg to be converted.[8]

Somewhat exaggerated stories of Henry's exploits were carried back home to England. He and his party did not embark back to England until February 1391, by which time, Henry was laden down with extra baggage: he had been given a number of falcons as presents by the grand master of the Teutonic Order, as well as two bears. The return journey took a month: he did not finally return to see his wife and new son Humphrey until March 1491. The following year, in the spring of 1392 and shortly after the birth of his first daughter, Blanche, he went back to Lithuania. His absence in Lithuania explains the gap of nearly two years between Humphrey and Blanche. Henry marked Blanche's birth in the manner typical to medieval aristocrats by spending money. He bought all four of his sons' new shirts made of costly 'cloth from Champagne. Henry and Thomas, at the tender ages of 5 and 4 received miniature livery collars as well. For John, now 3 years old, it must have been an exciting but perhaps rather overwhelming experience for the little boy who had perhaps only seen his father for perhaps one year of his short life.

After fifteen months at home, Henry's itchy feet got the better of him once again and in July 1392 he set off for Lithuania for the second time in two years. When he got there in September, he found out that the local prince was in the process of making peace with the master of the Teutonic Order and had dismissed all Western crusader knights. Instead of kicking up his heels in the Baltic, Henry decided to travel more and set off on 'the medieval equivalent of what would later become known as the grand tour'.[9] He visited Prague, followed by Vienna and finally Venice where he charted a vessel to travel to Jaffa: the port in the Holy Land. His intent was to undertake a pilgrimage to Jerusalem, and whilst he was there, he very likely visited the church of the Holy Sepulchre and the Mount of Olives. At some point, Henry also vowed to join any future crusade to retake the Holy Land: an ambition which many in Christendom still held even though the last of the crusades in the Middle East had ended in defeat more than a century earlier. With his pilgrimage finished, he returned home via Cyprus, Italy and France. On his travels, Henry made various contacts and established relationships with many notable people, having met the Holy Roman Emperor in Prague, and stayed with Albert of Hapsburg, Duke of Austria on his journey to the Holy Land. He also paid a visit to Sigismund, King of Hungary who later became Holy Roman Emperor.

On his return journey, he wined and dined with the grand master of the Knights Hospitaller and the king of Cyprus, James of Lusignan who gifted him a live leopard which he had to build a special enclosure for on the ship home. In Italy, he was hosted by Gian Galeazzo Visconti, Count of Vertus and Lord of Milan. Henry's uncle, Lionel of Antwerp had once been married to Gian Galeazzo's sister, Violante Visconti.[10] He finally returned to England more than a year after he had left in July 1393. Whilst there he also acquired a parrot given to him as a present for his wife Mary.

During Henry's travels, his wife and children moved around a lot. They spend much time residing with Henry Bolingbroke's father John of Gaunt. They stayed at his castles in Hereford and Leicester and also at the famous Bolingbroke Castle where their father had been born. Bolingbroke is named after the village in Lincolnshire which is now known as Old Bolingbroke and once consisted of a fortress with five D-shaped towers and a gatehouse enclosed in a curtain wall. It wasn't the largest, or most important of Gaunt's properties, but it was one he liked. Gaunt, as duke of Lancaster, had more lands and properties than his oldest son (not that Bolingbroke was poor) and it only made sense for him to host his son's family when his son was away from home, especially since he was also bankrolling Henry's travels and crusading endeavours.

By the summer of 1394, Henry had been home for a year, and his sixth child with Mary de Bohun was on the way. John was by then 5 and soon to be the middle of six children. However, the birth of his sister Philippa in the summer of 1394 was marked with tragedy, because his mother died shortly after the birth. Her death was a terrible and unexpected blow for Mary had been a great support to her husband throughout their marriage. She had given birth five or six times and survived, and they were both expecting another safe birth followed by a swift recovery. Mary was tragically young at only 24 or 25 years old when she died. Henry went into mourning for a full year after his beloved wife's death, suggesting there was a genuine bond of affection between them. Less than a year later he paid for black curtains to be hung around his four-poster bed, a sign that he was still in mourning. He also sent gifts to Leicester where his wife was buried in the Church of the Annunciation of Our Lady, Newarke.[11]

The year of Mary de Bohun's death, 1394, proved to be a year of tragedies for many in the English kingdom. In March, Constance, duchess of Lancaster, the second wife of John of Gaunt and stepmother of Henry of Derby, died. A few days after Mary de Bohun's passing, Anne of Bohemia the queen of England and beloved wife of King Richard II also died.[12] Anne died childless at the age of 28 after a short and unknown illness. If she and the king had had a child, the course of English history may have run very differently. Richard was inconsolable at the loss of his queen: he initially flew into a rage and reportedly ordered the palace of Sheen, in which she died, to be destroyed.[13] Later, he wrote to her kinsman Wilhelm, Duke of Guelders to postpone an official visit, saying 'the heaviest sadness and bitterness of heart' afflicted him. Even the chroniclers lamented the death of the beloved queen, saying that her death was a loss to the entire country and its people and not just to the king.[14]

The children of Henry, Earl of Derby were all about to face the upheaval of having to leave their childhood home, but at least they were able to stay together. The children went to live with their maternal grandmother, Joan de Bohun, dowager Countess of Hereford. It may seem strange that the sons of a nobleman went to live with a female relative after their mother died, but they were not wards of the crown since their father was still alive, was still one of the greatest lords in the country and held some of his late wife's lands by way of something called courtesy of England – something like a male version of dower. As such, Henry could still decide what to do with his children and where they could go: so, he sent them to their redoubtable grandmother. The six children lived with her, probably in Bytham Castle in Lincolnshire for at least one year, and probably longer. Joan was a Bohun by marriage but a Fitzalan by birth, a descendant of the Fitzalan earl of Arundel who had married Eleanor Plantagenet, the sister of Henry de Grosmont, Duke of Lancaster.

Chapter Two

Political Crisis

Henry's frequent absences between the births of his fourth and fifth children took him away from the court and from the centre of political events. Just a month or so before John's birth in 1389, King Richard II had reached his age of majority. This was the age of 21 for a male and for the king meant it was time to rule by himself and without the regency government that had previously been in place. Richard had become king in 1377 at the tender age of 8, and his majority came slightly early at 20.

He had known Henry Bolingbroke all his life, the pair were first cousins, and Henry was only two years older than Richard. It is beyond the scope of this book to examine their relationship in minute detail. All that is really relevant here were the dealings Bolingbroke had with the king between 1389 and 1399. Richard's own reign was a turbulent and sometimes troubled one: he had to head off The Peasant's Revolt in 1382 at the tender age of 13. In the winter of 1387–88, a group of lords known as the appellants rose in rebellion, demanding that the king impeach five of his closest advisors who they claimed were the cause of bad rule and tyranny which had beset the realm. These five were Michael de la Pole, Earl of Suffolk; Robert de Vere, Earl of Oxford (who Richard had given the title Duke of Ireland), Alexander Neville, Archbishop of York; Nicholas Brembre, a former major of London; and Robert Tresilian, a justice of the king's Bench. The Lords Appellant consisted of five lords, including Henry, Earl of Derby and Thomas of Woodstock, Duke of Gloucester, the youngest son of Edward III and uncle of the king. The other three were Richard Fitzalan, Earl of Arundel, Thomas de Beauchamp, Earl of Warwick, and Thomas de Mowbray, then earl of Nottingham. On their way to parliament they were apprehended by a force under the command of Robert de Vere, Earl of Oxford, one of the king's favourites who was a target of theirs. The Lords routed Vere's force in a skirmish at Radcot Bridge in Oxford, but he escaped.

For the following few months, the appellants set about destroying the royal favourites and their political enemies by legal and physical means, most notably during the so-called Merciless Parliament in the Spring of 1388. Most of the appellants' enemies had (wisely) disappeared, Michael de la Pole reportedly escaped to France disguised as a common servant. Hence, they had to target relatively minor figures such as Sir Simon Burley, formerly King Richard's tutor, Thomas Usk, a member of parliament, and many others. It has been proposed that the appellants deposed Richard II for a period of three days in the December of 1387 or early spring of 1388 with Gloucester temporarily withdrawing his fealty to the monarch and the appellants effectively ruling the country for that brief period. Rumours swirled that Gloucester intended to take the throne for himself, and he had to issue a formal statement denying it in parliament. What the appellants did was not just unprecedented in English history, their brutality and summary execution of opponents made them enemies. Most notable among them was the king himself. What he considered to be little better than the murder of his friend Simon Burley was to have a profound impact on the young monarch, and he bore a grudge against the appellants which would last for more than a decade.

In 1397, when he was 30 years old, Richard began to set in motion a plan to wreak vengeance on the appellants. On the eleventh of July he ordered the arrest of three of them: Arundel, Warwick and Gloucester. According to the chronicler Thomas Walsingham, the king had held a banquet and invited all three of them the day before but all had made excuses except the earl of Warwick. Warwick was by then aged 60, an old man by fourteenth-century standards. Richard went to get the earl of Gloucester himself, arriving at the duke's residence of Pleshey Castle early in the morning on the 11th. The castle had come into his possession since he married the eldest of the late Humphrey de Bohun's daughter Eleanor, although it was really part of his wife's inheritance. His marriage made him simultaneously the uncle and the brother-in-law of Henry Bolingbroke.

The king came so early that the earl and his family were woken up and the earl had to attend his king hastily dressed. At first, the king greeted him fondly, but his true intent soon became obvious and Gloucester was arrested with the chilling words from the king that he would be shown the same mercy as he had granted to Simon Burley years earlier. Thomas, Duke of Gloucester was sent to Calais to be imprisoned and await trail on the allegation of 'treason'. Richard, it appears wanted to put the three men on trial for what had happened nine years earlier arguing that they had abandoned their allegiance and risen against their king.

It seems bizarre to have sent him such a long way, but kings did this with important prisoners if they wanted to avoid an outcry or place them in the hands of a person who they especially trusted. The captain of Calais was Thomas Mowbray, first duke of Norfolk. Parliament was opened on 17 September to the shocking news that Gloucester had died in Calais before he could be brought to trial. It is generally held that he was murdered, probably on the orders of Richard himself. Richard would probably have never been successful in having Gloucester condemned for treason, but nobody could have touched the son of a king without his assent, so his death most likely falls on Richard's shoulders. Who actually carried out the alleged murder is unknown: it may have been the agent Thomas Mowbray, shockingly one of the other five original appellants. He and Henry Bolingbroke were involved in the proceedings against their former compatriot in 1397–98 and these were events which would soon come back to bite them.

Despite Gloucester's death, parliament proceeded against the other two accused. Warwick was sentenced to lifelong exile on the Isle of Man which many thought would not be a very long time considering his age. Nevertheless, the elderly man had been forced to demean himself to begging for mercy in parliament and the king was supposedly moved by his tears. Although, the chronicler Froissart says that the earl of Salisbury pleaded for Warwick to be spared execution. Executing an old man such as Warwick would not have done Richard's reputation any favours, although by this point, he does not seem to have cared very much.

The earl of Arundel was not so lucky. He was brought to trial before the Lords on 21 September and made a 'spirited and articulate' defence in front of his peers: several of whom were his relatives including his nephew Thomas Holland, Earl of Kent. He even called his called his main accuser, Henry Bolingbroke, a liar to his face.[1] He was, of course, convicted and was taken to execution the very same day. He was, shockingly sentenced to be hanged, drawn and quartered, although Richard commuted it to beheading. It was the first time in decades that an English nobleman had been condemned and executed and perhaps the first time in living memory that a nobleman had been executed for an offence committed nearly ten years earlier for which he had previously been pardoned. Arundel was escorted to the place of execution by his nephew Thomas Holland, the earl of Kent and duke of Norfolk who was, in fact, none other than his son-in-law and the father of his grandchildren. It was an ignominious end to the Lords Appellant: that two of them ended up presiding over the trials of another two for treason and the fifth may have been murdered by one of his fellows.

Richard had made certain to pardon him and the remaining living appellant, Norfolk. But, could the king's pardons really be trusted in light of the events which had taken place? Richard did one more thing in 1397 which may have created cause for concern. He seemed to be looking back with something like nostalgia to the reign of Edward II, his great-grandfather who had died seventy years earlier. Arundel had been executed on 21 September, the anniversary of the day of Edward II's murder. Richard also decided to declare the sentence upon the Despensers: the father and son duo who had once been favourites of Edward II and had been declared traitors in 1321.

Edward II had been considered a tyrant by some, and the closing years of his reign were a dangerous precedent to look back to with apparent fondness.

Another act was for Richard to promote some of his favoured nobles. Henry Bolingbroke was promoted from earl of Derby to duke of Hereford. This title was apparently an elevated version of the title late wife's father, Humphrey de Bohun had once held that of earl of Hereford. Alongside him, John Holland was made duke of Exeter and Thomas Holland, duke of Surrey. Ralph Neville, previously a Northern baron, albeit one of considerable means and power was made earl of Northumberland and the younger brother of Henry Percy, Thomas Percy was made earl of Worcester. Before 1397 the title of duke had been rare in England: and the title was generally reserved for the sons of the king. The new ones created by Richard were dubbed the *duketti* or 'little Dukes'.

In 1397, Henry Bolingbroke and Mowbray were still in Richard's good books and had escaped the consequences of their involvement with the appellants. Henry must have felt that he was off the hook after parliament wrapped up the closing days of September 1397. He was wrong. Early the following year he met Norfolk, and the duke alleged that several lords were plotting to murder Henry and his father the duke of Lancaster. There are various accounts of the claims Norfolk made and who was involved, and although they might have seemed far-fetched to Henry, they underscore the prevailing atmosphere of the royal court in 1398–99. One of fear, suspicion and paranoia: whispers and rumours of treachery and murder were rife: even the king himself could not be trusted.

In July, the king summoned both Henry Bolingbroke and the duke of Norfolk to see him. He had learned of the conversation between the two men in February or March and Norfolk claimed that he had plotted to set a trap and possibly kill John of Gaunt, Duke of Lancaster. Norfolk was remanded in custody in the King's Wardrobe: a building located near Blackfriars. In July, the two were supposed to appear before the king by the second of September because their grievances were considered to be a matter which pertained to him. Each of the Lords was basically accusing the other of treason; Henry alleging that Norfolk had been involved in the murder of the duke of Gloucester. King Richard arranged for them to settle the matter in a judicial duel to be held at Coventry on the sixteenth of September 1398. Judicial duels, sometimes referred to as Trial by Combat, were relatively uncommon in England by the fourteenth century. In fact, it was made into an international spectacle with many people including foreign dignitaries, expected to turn out to watch two of the most prominent lords of the realm, engage in single combat. Word of it even reached the Continent when Henry sent gifts to the heralds of the king of Portugal and the duke of Burgundy, and the duke of Brittany's herald was supposed to preside over the event. Giangelezzo Visconti, Duke of Milan sent Henry Bolingbroke a fine, Italian-made suit of armour for the occasion. He didn't give this gift because he simply liked Henry: he was touting his sister as a possible wife for him.

On the morning of 16 September, everyone converged upon Coventry. The duel would probably have been held in a field near or outside the town in a specially constructed area with lists such as those used for jousting and seating for spectators. Both combatants dressed in 'a doublet of red Kendal cloth' (a short tunic which would have been worn over the armour) and with twenty retainers in tow who were just as splendidly attired as the combatants marched into the lists.[2] Amidst the dramatic fanfare, the herald of the duke of Brittany made a signal to stop the duel. Shakespeare suggests that the king himself held up his arms, but it was more likely a herald formally interrupted the duel before it started in this way, when the two men were preparing for combat.

The two were once again summoned separately into the royal presence: whereupon the angry king chastised them both:

> letting it be known that he wished to stand between them
> and that he was highly displeased by all they had said
> and done, which were not things to be easily forgiven.

He then sent the Constable and the Steward of England
with four other noblemen to obtain a promise from the
two adversaries that they would obey any order that the
king gave them. Both pledged themselves to do so and
their promise was reported to the king in the presence of
the whole court ... .[3]

The king thereupon passed judgement on the two errant nobles.
Norfolk was exiled from England for life for 'he has sown dissension
in this country and uttered words of which there is no other evidence
but his own account of them'.[4] Henry was similarly ordered to abjure
the realm for ten years. Some may ask why Norfolk was given a
more severe penalty. It is probably because he had instigated some of
the allegations against Henry and even the king, and because of the
still lingering suspicions about his involvement in the death of the
duke of Gloucester. Unlike what Shakespeare said, Norfolk was not
an old man and Henry a young one; there was only a year between
them. Norfolk was 33 and Bolingbroke 32 years of age.

Both were given several weeks to prepare, set their affairs in order
and leave the country. Norfolk had a great deal of money put away
with Italian bankers and would have been able to live comfortably on
the Continent. Of course, it would have been painful for the duke to
leave behind his home and everyone he had ever known including his
wife and five children who ranged in age from a new-born infant to his
14-year-old firstborn son and heir. Mowbray set off from Lowestoft
on the nineteenth of September. He went first to Calais, which he had
formally been captain of and from thence headed to Venice. It seems
that he was planning to go on a pilgrimage to the Holy Land from
there, but he never actually made it: he died of plague in Venice on
22 September 1399 and was buried (perhaps) in St Mark's Church.

Henry Bolingbroke was, of course, also exiled. He similarly
had to bid farewell to his family. His sons were 11, 10 and 9 and
almost 8 respectively. The girls Philippa and Blanche were 6 and 4.
Kathryn Warner suggests that Bolingbroke actually took his second

son, Thomas, aged 10 with him into exile. By this time, he was already apparently his father's favourite even though he was not the eldest. Henry had suffered a lot of ill health in his childhood and was thought to have been quite weak as a baby: and that might have been the reason why his brother Thomas became their faither's favourite. Another reason might be that Richard took the young Henry to court with him, and so his father was not allowed or able to take his eldest son with him. Although Carleton Williams said that the young John resided at Bytham or Framlingham Castle for most of this time, that may not have been the case. The three older Lancastrian boys were moved around a lot in their early days, and John may have spent much of 1398–99 in London with his new tutor, a man by the name of Thomas Rothwell.[5]

Bolingbroke's father John of Gaunt, Duke of Lancaster advised him to head either for Paris, Spain or Portugal. His half-sister Catalina lived in Spain and his full sister Blanche was married to the ruler of Portugal. He opted for Paris, where he was treated like an honoured guest and might have stayed were it not for what happened a few months later. In February 1399, John of Gaunt, Duke of Lancaster died. His son's exile seems to have been what broke the spirit of the formidable John of Gaunt who had once taken the helm of government and had been at the heart of power for so many decades.

As soon as Henry left England in October, the duke's health began to deteriorate, an event which would not have been helped by the fact that Richard reportedly wrote to the king of France asking him not to treat Bolingbroke so favourably. He had been treated with great honour at the French court.[6] Although Gaunt had other sons, the departure of his eldest son and heir from the country and the prospect of not seeing him again was apparently too much for him. In his last days he made a will in which he bequeathed a golden cup to the young John.[7] This is interesting because John is the only one of Gaunt's grandchildren who is mentioned in the will, let alone left a bequest. Was John Gaunt's favourite grandchild? It is entirely possible, especially since he was the one named after Gaunt. A golden goblet would have been a valuable gift for the 9-year-old, and although he might not have had much use for it at the time, he no doubt appreciated the gift from his namesake grandfather in later years.

John of Gaunt passed away in his bed at his castle in Leicester on the third of February and was buried in the old St Paul's Cathedral in London the following month. Henry heard about it and paid for masses for his father's soul in France. Nothing might have changed were it not for Richard's actions shortly after Gaunt's death: he extended Henry's exile to make it lifelong and then seized his inheritance, the Duchy of Lancaster and all the lands which belonged to the late duke. This was the inheritance which was supposed to have gone to Gaunt's son, and Richard had previously promised him that he would have livery of his lands once his father died and that doing fealty for them could be delayed until his return from exile. Richard's act was both curious and dangerous: he must have known it would provoke a reaction, but perhaps he saw it as an assertion of his power and a means of proverbially 'killing' the last remaining appellant. However, there is some that he did not intend the confiscation to be permanent, and even though he was granting some of the Duchy of Lancaster lands to others he was only doing it for a temporary period and intended to give them back to Bolingbroke when he returned. This is unlikely though: it is more likely Richard saw the matter of the Lancastrian inheritance as a way to deprive Bolingbroke of any future resources, and use them for his own purposes.

Sir William Bagot, a servant of Richard claimed that he sent a messenger to Henry in France, warning him that the king, his cousin, was now an implacable enemy and that he should use force to recover his rights. In the spring of 1399, Richard prepared for a visit to Ireland: one which was brought on by the death of his cousin (and once his heir) Roger Mortimer during a skirmish the year before. He left in late May. At the same time, Henry was making plans in France. Plans to return to England. He was joined by the son and heir of the earl of Arundel, and his relative the exiled archbishop of Canterbury, Thomas Arundel.

In early July, according to tradition, a small ship appeared bobbing off the coast of Yorkshire: it landed at Ravenspur on the East Riding coast. When Henry landed, he initially protested loyalty to the king saying that he only wanted to reclaim the lands of the Duchy of Lancaster. It would be a be a strategy that was used by many others in future decades, but Henry started it. Later versions say that as Henry moved through Yorkshire men flocked to his cause: we know that he went to his castles at Pickering and Knaresborough. Yorkshire was the Lancastrian power base and when Henry arrived a series of lords who held lands in the North joined with him, including Henry Percy, Earl of Northumberland and Ralph Neville, Earl of Westmorland. From Yorkshire he moved South and arrived at Warwick Castle by 24 July. Allegedly, Henry was greeted with celebration on his progress through the country: at least that is what Henry wanted people to believe as he sought to present himself as the champion of the people who would bring peace, justice and good rule.

In the summer months of 1399, England was almost in a state of unofficial civil war. Obviously not everyone supported Henry and for a time, Edmund of Langley, Duke of York, who was the regent of England in the king's absence began mustering troops to oppose Henry in the South. Other loyalists operated in the South and the Midlands: orders were issued to prepare Nottingham and Rockborough Castle for defence against Henry in the event of a siege. On 27 July, York met with his nephew Henry before the high altar of a church and there he agreed that Henry's cause was just and not to oppose him. Some say that Henry made a promise that he wasn't going to claim the crown, but there doesn't seem to be any specific evidence for this, and it is likely York had already guessed what his intentions were. The capitulation of the regent spelt the end for the loyalist cause, and many of those still loyal to Richard were arrested the following day.

Richard finally returned to England in mid-to late July, having heard news that his cousin was taking power and many of his lords had abandoned him. Not all though: he travelled through Wales and the earl of Salisbury rallied to him. Although the loyalists had raised a large army by the time the king returned, many of their troops had deserted or even gone over to Henry's side: because of lack of action or pay. Richard had taken two youngsters with him to Ireland when he left: one of them was Henry of Monmouth, the 12-year-old son of Henry Bolingbroke and the other was his young cousin, Humphrey of Buckingham, the 18-year-old son of Thomas of Woodstock. The two boys were officially the wards of the king, but it is not hard to see them as hostages since they were the sons and heirs of two of the Lords Appellant who had been deemed enemies of the king. He didn't treat either of them badly, in fact, the young Henry of Monmouth had been knighted shortly after the king set out along with five or six other noblemen's sons who were in his party.[8] It is possible King Richard planned to take the boy with him, since he had been contributing to his upkeep for some time beforehand and he did not, in fact, take Henry to Ireland as a hostage after all, but was instead undertaking the normal medieval practice of taking a young nobleman's son on a military expedition.

When Richard returned to England, he reportedly ensured the young Henry and Humphrey were safely ensconced in Trim Castle in the English-ruled part of Ireland. This suggests the boys were, at least by that time, viewed as potentially valuable hostages, with Henry having some potential to be used as leverage to ensure his father's loyalty. It must have been a frightening experience for the youngster, although Henry would look back on his time with King Richard with some fondness in later years.

Richard travelled through Wales on his return seeking to reunite with members of his council to learn about Henry Bolingbroke's movements and make plans. He sent loyal allies (including the son of the duke of York) to mobilise troops but then made the fateful decision to ride alone through Wales, abandoning an army which had been raised for him to join up with the earl of Salisbury in Chester. Although Salisbury was unflinchingly loyal and received the king, his army of 40,000 men had melted away upon hearing that Bolingbroke had captured Bristol. Richard now had no army, which would have been his best hope of wresting control of the country away from his recalcitrant cousin.

Running out of options, Richard went to Conway Castle in North Wales, where he decided to try to negotiate with his adversaries. In the meantime, Chester fell to him. At Conwy, Richard met with the earl of Northumberland who was acting as Henry's emissary: accounts of what passed between them are heavily slanted in favour of the Lancastrian regime but they supposedly involved Northumberland assuring Richard of his cousin's love and asking him to restore Bolingbroke to the lands and titles. By 18 August, Richard was only 35 miles away from Conwy in the company of Northumberland, who sent a message to Henry saying that Richard had been captured and was in his power.[9] It was at Flint that Richard finally met Henry two days after his arrival and it was there that sources favourable to Henry claim that Richard submitted to his cousin and agreed to let him help rule the kingdom. This was not a formal deposition: yet: that happened when Henry took Richard with him to London and summoned a parliament (himself!) for the thirtieth of September.

Richard was allegedly taken to the Tower of London, and around 29 or 30 September he was brought before the Lords. *The Traison et Mort* says:

> Lancaster entered, he found there already seated all the prelates of the kingdom, The Duke came in state thus and … his four sons walking before him; and his two brothers, and the three Dukes, of Surrey, Aumarle, and Exeter who all wore his livery, walking arm in arm after him. And when the duke had entered, Sir Thomas Percy, bearing a white rod in his hand, sat down right before the

duke and cried out 'Long live Henry of Lancaster, King of England.'[10]

Was it really that easy? Did all the Lords really just accept Henry just like that? Well, the same source does recount the proceedings against Richard in the Lords, but not the way in which Henry had been working on Richard for the better part of a month before that. The former king as his captive probably feared for his life. The *Traison* mentions that people had already been calling for his execution, but it also contains an extensive account of how the bishop of Carlisle defended Richard and demanded that he should appear before the Lords in full. Carlisle was reportedly arrested for his efforts: although the Lords' calls for Aumerle to be immediately executed were ignored.

The next day when the Lords was in session Henry was proclaimed king and his coronation was held less than two weeks later.

Part Two

SON OF A KING
1399–1413

Chapter Three

Usurpation

O n the 30 September 1399, the young John of Lancaster's life changed forever. He was brought to London along with all his siblings (including young Henry, returned from Ireland) on the 12 October to watch the coronation of the father he had probably not seen in more than a year, and now his father was being crowned as king. The coronation of Henry IV was held on exactly one year to the day that Henry had said goodbye to his father and just before he had left England for exile.

On the day before, the eleventh of October, young John was knighted, possibly in the presence of Richard, who they were now no longer supposed to call the king. Then the following day, his oldest brother was made prince of Wales: the title traditionally given to the heir to the throne. The last prince of Wales had been Edward of Woodstock, known as The Black Prince, and the father of Richard II who had died many years before Henry of Bolingbroke (now King Henry IV's) children were born.

At his father's coronation, the newly knighted 10-year-old and his brothers were invested into the newly founded Order of the Bath. His knighting was part of an elaborate ceremony which involved taking a bath to symbolically wash away his sins and then walked in procession to St John's Chapel in in the Tower of London to keep a vigil for the night before the knighting ceremony. It would have been a long night for a 10-year-old, although perhaps exceptions were made for younger people, and they didn't have to stay at vigil all night. The knighting of his sons at his coronation illustrates how Henry intended the new Lancastrian monarchy to be a family affair with his sons, half-brothers and other relatives involved in the government. Henry was soon to discover that he could not simply usurp an anointed king and carry on as though nothing had happened.

Barely two weeks after his coronation there was drama in parliament when John Bagot, a close aide and servant of Richard was brought to trial and ended up very publicly accusing the duke of Aumerle, Henry's cousin, of the murder of the duke of Gloucester. Others then followed suit and a riot almost ensued. Matters were only taken into hand when Henry begged, threatened and cajoled the Lords and finally promised to put Aumerle and the other so-called counter appellants on trial.[1] If was an embarrassing and fraught situation for the king which served to demonstrate the spectre of the past had not gone away. Feeling he needed to be conciliatory, the Lords who had moved against him in 1397 were merely demoted from the titles Richard II had given them and stripped of the ill-gotten gains of land that had been taken from Henry and Gloucester two years earlier. Richard II it was decided at the same time was to be imprisoned in the Tower of London for life. Henry very much didn't want to kill his cousin and didn't know what the constitutional position was for putting an anointed king on trial.

Henry was about to learn that being so merciful came at a high cost. Before the new year of 1400 had even dawned, several prominent nobles began formulating a plot to murder Henry and his sons and restore Richard to the throne. Their plan apparently involved a plot to sneak into Windsor Castle during the Christmas festivities and may have involved the complicity of Richard II's young queen, Isabella. The main lords involved were John Holland, Duke of Exeter, the half-brother of Richard II, and Thomas Holland, Earl of Huntingdon, his nephew, the earl of Salisbury and Thomas Despenser. The plot was betrayed to Henry IV by an unknown party before it was carried out: tradition has it that this party was Edmund of Langley, Duke of York or his son, Edward of Norwich also known as the earl of Aumerle. Once the conspirators knew the game was up, they fled in separate directions and all were punished brutally. John Holland tried to escape the country, but ended up in Essex, where he fell into the hands of Joan de Bohun, the mother-in-law of Henry. Joan promptly had him executed. She may even have sent word to her son-in-law to ask what to do with the captured nobleman beforehand. Henry had no issue with Holland's execution, despite the fact that he was married to Henry's younger sister Elizabeth. Perhaps he thought that Holland's betrayal outweighed any personal or familial connections, but Joan was to prove that those connections could be strong when underscored by loyalty. She was one of Henry's most erstwhile allies.

Thomas Holland and John Montague, Earl of Salisbury (once the young Henry of Monmouth's guardian and mentor) were caught in Cirencester and beheaded by what essentially amounted to a mob lynching and a similar fate befell Thomas Despenser in Bristol. The heads of two of the men involved in the rising were sent to Henry in baskets: a gruesome sign that he was now safe from the threat. The event known as the Epiphany Rising in the early weeks of 1400 also sealed the fate of the unfortunate Richard II. Had the Lords not rebelled, Henry might have been content to leave the former king a prisoner, but people conducting rebellions in his name was always inevitable. By the end of February 1400, Richard, who had been moved to Pontefract Castle in Yorkshire was dead. We don't know exactly how the former king died, but it is generally posited that he was starved to death, or even that he starved himself to death when he heard about the failure of the Epiphany Rising.

Traison et Mort has a more colourful story in which Henry dispatched a young esquire by the name of Peter Exton to kill Richard. This account tells of how Richard defended himself manfully against Exton and a band of seven armed men he brought with him before Exton struck the former king over the head.[2] This account, though, is unlikely to be true. Although it is very likely Henry did have Richard killed, he would not have wanted the act performed in such a clumsy and brutal manner which would have made it obvious that the former king had been murdered. Even when he was deposed, ordering such an act would have made Henry look bad. Whatever happened, Richard was dead by the 14 February 1400 at Pontefract. His body was brought down to London for public viewing in St Paul's Cathedral and was later buried in the relatively obscure location of Langley Priory in Herefordshire. Langley was apparently chosen because Richard's older brother who had died in childhood had also been buried there.

For the next several years, Henry was never entirely free of conspiracies and plots against him. The deposition of Richard II as popular as it might have been at the time, would hang over Henry for the rest of his natural life. John, only 10 when his father took crown, was now third in line to the throne. He seems to have spent the two or three years after the usurpation completing his education. He may have spent time studying at Oxford University. The idea of a pre-teen studying at Oxford may seem strange to us, but this wasn't an uncommon aspect children's education in the later medieval period. It may have been something akin to going to high school. His brother Henry also attended Queen's College Oxford at the tender age of 11 but may have only stayed for a few months as whatever studies he undertook were interrupted by his father's exile, upon which he was hastily yanked out of Oxford and taken to the royal court.

John's pre-teen years were also a time when he was granted a number of lands including various parcels of land which had once belonged to Richard II and those confiscated from lords who had been loyal to him. It seems strange to us for a child so young to be given land, money or titles but it was considered perfectly normal by fifteenth-century standards for a boy of noble birth and especially a king's son. medieval nobles did not have the time to take care of the day-to-day needs of their offspring and so setting them up with their own household made perfect sense. By 1400 the young John already had his own household staff, including several priests, a chaplain and musicians who served under a dean of the chapel. He would also have had other, secular staff and so his household probably consisted of several dozen individuals, possibly up to 100. They would have travelled with him and so, as he got older, we must imagine him travelling with his entire household when he went to the North or to London.

In 1400, John was given 'the town and castle of Briavels in the forest of Dean' which had once belonged to his Uncle Thomas, duke of Gloucester. He was also given the lordship of Ware in Hertfordshire which brought him an income of some £120 per year. All these were fairly normal grants of lands which became vacant or available due to the deaths (or sometimes the forfeitures) of previous landholders. It seems strange to use for a child so young to be given land, money or titles but it was considered perfectly normal by fifteenth-century standards for a boy of noble birth and especially a king's son. He was also appointed to the royal council, a small group of hand-picked men who advised the king. The 11-year-old was not expected to offer advice or counsel to his father: he and his brother were put on the council to learn by listening and observing.

In 1403, the tides of political events would once again sweep up the young John. Since the start of his reign, Henry IV had to keep many of the lords and nobles of the realm on his side, and his reign was to be marked by near-constant rebellion. The early years saw the ascendancy of the Percy family who had held the title of earls of Northumberland since the 1370s. Henry taking the throne led to a resurgence of problems on the Northern border with Scotland and rebel sentiments in Wales. There even emerged a pretender to the crown, in the form of a fake Richard II in Scotland. Whilst Henry Percy, Earl of Northumberland spent most of his time in London as a member of the royal council, his son also called Henry Percy, but more commonly known by his nickname of Hotspur, was a soldier. He spent most of his time patrolling and defending the so-called marches of Scotland and Wales. Unlike his portrayal in Shakespeare's play, Hotspur was not some green youth, but a seasoned warrior in his thirties.

The Percys had some very interesting family connections. By marriage, Hotspur was related to the Mortimer family: his wife Elizabeth was the sister of Roger Mortimer who had died in 1398 and had once been the successor of Richard II. His brother-in-law Edmund Mortimer (called Edmund Mortimer Senior to distinguish him from the son of Roger of the same name) was captured in Wales by Owain Glyn Dŵr, the Welsh nobleman who was the leading figure in an uprising against Henry and the English at the beginning of the fifteenth century. Edmund's period in captivity cannot have been too strenuous, since he went on to marry Glyn Dŵr's daughter in late 1402.

This made for an interesting situation since Hotspur was one of Henry's leading lieutenants in Wales. The relationship between Henry IV and the Percys took a turn for the worse in 1401–02 due to a variety of factors, including the king's refusal to allow Hotspur to ransom an extremely valuable Scottish prisoner and disagreements over royal policy in Wales and Scotland. Hotspur wanted a more conciliatory approach towards men like Glyn Dŵr when the king took a much harder line.

Still, Henry breathed more easily for the remainder of 1402 and into the next year. In early 1403, he married for the second time. It had been almost eight years since the death of Mary de Bohun, the mother of his children. The woman he married in February 1403 was named Joan of Navarre, a noblewoman of Basque extraction who had previously been wed to the duke of Brittany with whom she had several children.

It is likely that she met Henry at some point during his exile in France, but they delayed marriage for nearly three years, partly on the grounds of French opposition to their match. On the twenty-sixth of February, she was crowned queen of England, as Mary de Bohun might have been had she survived. Henry was nearly 36 years old, and Joan was 34, it was the second marriage for both of them and they both had children by their first spouses. By fifteenth-century standards it was considered unlikely that a woman of 34 could still have children, but not impossible. It is likely Henry married Joan for personal reasons, perhaps even love.[3] It had been almost ten years since the death of his wife, and although it is true that Henry was known to have been faithful to both his spouses, Henry did have at least one illegitimate child who was born in the interval between the death of Mary and his marriage to Joan. His bastard son was known as Edmund Laborde, and his mother was sadly unknown. Edmund seems to have been put into the church, the typical fate of 'spare' children at this time, especially since Henry did not want his bastard son to be a potential threat to the inheritance to any of his legitimate children.

Although it would have been advantageous for to make an alliance with a foreign realm, he had no need for an heir with four healthy sons. Joan's own son, in turn, was the future duke of Brittany. Henry's boys by then ranged between 12 to 16 years of age (and Edmund may have only been a toddler). By all accounts, Joan developed a good relationship with her four stepsons in these early years after her marriage although they didn't always see very much of her. Later, when the reconquest of France became a priority for Henry's eldest son and heir, Joan's relationship with all of her stepsons became more strained because her children by her first marriage fought against England.

On the 01 April the king decided to replace Hotspur as his lieutenant on the Marches of Wales. His replacement was his own son, the 16-year-old Henry of Monmouth now prince of Wales. It didn't go down well to expect seasoned warriors to answer to a teenage boy.[4] Of course, it also helped that the office of lieutenant came with an annual wage of over £8,000, so losing it was a financial blow as well. Despite his age, the young Prince Henry did a good job: his forces relieved two castles which were under siege and then went on to ravage two of Glyn Dŵr's estates. Medieval 16-year-olds could be formidable military leaders and commanders in their own right, and the Henry appeared determined to emulate his famous forbear, the Black Prince.

By July 1403, Hotspur decided he had had enough. He marched on Chester and announced that Richard II was still alive: anyone who wanted to restore the old king and overthrow Henry, it was proclaimed should gather at Sandiway. Many went, although they did not of course meet Richard and instead found themselves recruited into a rebel army by Hotspur who was probably already working by collusion with his brother-in-law Edmund Mortimer and Glyn Dŵr. He was also joined by his uncle, Thomas Percy, Earl of Worcester, making the rebellion a family affair. Glyn Dŵr, who was supposed to join Percy's army was actually marching his forces in the opposite direction, but Percy's forces were buoyed by his uncle and by his father's attempts to encourage the king to remain in London.

The king decided not to. He made the fateful decision to go north and heard about Hotspur's revolt when he reached Nottingham. Unprepared for the king's advance, Hotspur abandoned his plans to attack Prince Harry in Shrewsbury and moved his forces a few miles northwest. The armies came within sight of each other on Saturday 21 July and there were several hours of negotiations which proved to be fruitless. The proceeding military engagement was known as the Battle of Shrewsbury and is considered by some at least to have been the first battle in the Wars of the Roses: it was certainly the first in which 'ranks of England and Welsh archers were pitted against one another' on each side 'and would long be remembered as one of the bloodiest battles fought on English soil' largely as a result of that fact.[5] The 16-year-old prince of Wales and the future King Henry V of England was commanding his father's rearguard in what may well have been his first taste of real battle. At first, Hotspur had the advantage, and his troops sent the king's vanguard breaking and running. They also managed to kill the man leading the royal vanguard, the earl of Stafford who was only 25 years old. The king moved to a safer position, but according to the official sources the young prince of Wales fought on 'leading the royalist vanguard' in a heroic counterattack despite being struck in the face with an arrow.

In the melee which followed the prince's counterattack, Hotspur was killed: ironically in a similar manner to how the prince of Wales sustained his injury. He was, according to tradition, shot through the throat with an arrow. Cries of his death caused the rebel army to break ranks and run and as was all too typical with battles, fleeing men were cut down mercilessly in the rout by pursuing enemies. Casualties of the Battle of Shrewsbury were high though on both sides, and it the immediate aftermath it was thought unlikely the prince of Wales would survive. Only the capable ministration of the surgeon John Bradmore saved him. This arrow embedded itself in his cheek and penetrated nearly 6 inches. Although he survived it would have left Henry with a horrible scar.[6]

Bradmore was a trained surgeon, but he was also in trouble with the law. Before entering King Henry's service he had been convicted of coin forgery which was a capital offense in medieval England. He was luckily pardoned, possibly because the king saw his potential and hired him. In 1403, he would have been glad of the fact. Bradmore left behind a unique and fascinating account of the surgery he performed on the young Henry, which dispels some of the myths about medieval surgeons having been incompetent butchers who were more likely to kill their patients than anything else. After the Battle of Shrewsbury, he described how the prince was taken to Kenilworth and how after enlarging the wound he:

> I made new tongs small and hollow to the size of an arrow, and in the middle of the tongs entered a certain screw … The which tongs I put in transversely in the same manner that the arrow first entered then I also put the screw in the middle and at length the tongs entered the cavity of the arrowhead and then moving it to and for, little by little, with God's help, I extracted the arrowhead.[7]

After removing the arrowhead, Bradmore washed out the wound with white wine, and filing the cavity with wads of flax soaked in a flax soaked in 'a cleansing ointment, which he had prepared … bread sops, barley, honey and turpentine oil'.[8] It took the prince the better part of a month to recover, but it is speculated that he may have been out of action for up to a year. Which makes the fact that he continued fighting after being hit at Shrewsbury even more remarkable: he must have been in agony the whole time.

In the aftermath of Shrewsbury, the not so lucky Hotspur's head was put on a spike atop the main gate of the city. His uncle, the earl of Worcester was executed. Deprived of the main defenders of the Welsh and Scottish borders, the king needed to find replacements. It was here that the young John came in. Not long after his fourteenth birthday he was appointed warden of the east March, responsible for the defence of the extensive borderlands of Scotland. He and the trusted Ralph Neville, earl of Westmorland who was married to Henry IV's sister Joan Beaufort, were to share the Marches between them.[9] Westmorland was to be John's mentor and ally. Westmorland was a seasoned soldier in his forties, and a veteran of campaigns on the border. He was the best possible choice to work alongside the young Bedford. This appointment in 1403 was really what marked the start of John's military training and career. He did not know it at the time, but John would spend the better part of a decade patrolling the northern borderlands of England protecting and defending his father's realm in the company of the earl of Westmorland.

Even though the earl of Northumberland was still alive, he had been stripped of the role of warden of the west and western March following the Battle of Shrewsbury but was restored to all his other lands. The king had wanted a harsher punishment for the earl, but it was not supported and everyone realised that stripping him of his lands or something worse could cause instability on the important northern border. Perhaps even another invasion with collusion of the Scots. Henry could not afford that, so he gave Northumberland his lands back, but put his son in co-charge of defence of the northern border.

The 14-year-old John was thrown into the proverbial deep end. Here was a young man who had been born and raised in the Midlands heartlands of the Lancastrians and was suddenly thrust into to the cut-throat world of the northern border and the power politics of the northern lords who were like kings in their own right. In 1404 John was also appointed constable of England. This was a position which allowed him to judge people suspected of certain crimes and felonies basically on the spot of that was necessary. Especially useful considering how the border country was notoriously lawless at the best of times.[10]

This move suggests John was a remarkably astute and capable young man who realised what was needed of him and sought to obtain everything he needed to do it. The king's writ was hard to enforce in the North and many were still loyal to Henry Percy. There were cases of Percy loyalists refusing to hand over castles. He and Westmorland still had to deal with the aforementioned Percy loyalists, alongside the perpetual threat of Scottish incursions over the border. Westmorland was far from conciliatory and was said to be very heavy handed with Percy retainers, a position which arose perhaps, from personal animosity. Northumberland and Westmorland were the two greatest northern lords, and the rivalry between them proved to be especially bitter when Westmorland was given power.

Westmorland seemed determined to show his hatred towards his rival as well as any Percy retainers and his young protégé was caught in the middle. Although he was the king's son, John had little real authority in his own right, alongside an older and more experienced commander but probably faced much frustration when he had to contend with the problems caused by Westmorland's personal animosity. Of course, he was loyal to his father, and the impressionable young man may well have hated Hotspur and even blamed the man for almost killing his older brother. We don't know if Westmorland's personal opinions rubbed off on him or if John started to suspect that maybe he was going too far in antagonising the northern knights and lords who were in the circle of the earl of Northumberland.

John's appointment proved to be timely, for in early 1405, the earl of Northumberland started making moves to oust Westmorland from power and even hatched a plot to seize his rival when he was staying with a friend in Durham. The earl somehow learned of the plot and escaped. With that failed, he seized the knight who King Henry had sent north to parley with him, and then fortified the city of Berwick-upon-Tweed as well as several of his castles. In May, John and Westmorland arrived at Topcliffe in North Yorkshire to quell an uprising by a series of local knights who had gathered perhaps as many as 6,000 followers and retainers together to seek redress for grievances. One of the knights was one Sir Colville del Dale, no doubt the man who inspired the knight named Sir Coleville of the Dale in Shakespeare's *Henry IV* (Part II). The ringleaders were captured and many of the others dispersed.[11]

John and Westmorland had an uncanny knack for learning of events and plots before they came to anything, or just happening up turn up at the right time to stamp out uprisings. This strongly suggests they had put together a network of spies or informants who operated in the household of the Percys and their adherents. Or the spies worked for the king and had been operating for some time because Henry distrusted the earl of Northumberland. John may even have had contacts within the central government itself, because he received intelligence of John, lord Bardolph a close ally and adherent of Percy leaving the Lords secretly and travelling north in early May 1405, before the attempt to abduct Westmorland was made.[12] Fortunately, we have a letter written by John to his father in May 1405 in which John stated the source of his information. Writing from Durham, he stated that the mayor of Newcastle informed him that a man of the town had seen Lord Bardolph in the city of Berwick 'with a great company of Scots' and in the company of the earl of Northumberland. Bardolph was meant to be in London, at the royal council, and although he only had a second or third hand account, John considered it serious enough to inform his father.[13]

It is easy for modern historians with the benefit of hindsight to look at end past in a very simplistic way, and attribute actions to very simple motives. To assume that this or that rebellion happened because someone was disliked or that a person's loyalty was determined by which country or region they name came from. Not everyone from north-eastern England owed their first loyalty to the Percys. As we can see from the letter, a person in Newcastle-upon-Tyne considered the presence of Northumberland, Bardolf and a number of Scots in the city to be sufficient cause for concern, that they saw fit to inform the authorities.

We know Henry V used spies to keep an eye on powerful nobles and their regional adherents, especially in the early part of his reign when he was beset with plots, uprisings and opposition from almost every corner so why not his father? We know that John and Westmorland were in constant communication with King Henry who had been at Worcester throughout May of 1405, and they were probably taking orders and directions from him, as well as exchanging information.

Coleville and his compatriots were almost certainly acting at the behest of the earl of Northumberland, and although their abortive uprising was nipped in the bud, the underlying tide of dissent and rebellion ran more deeply. Richard Scrope, the archbishop of York preached a sermon on 17 May, and together with the young Thomas Mowbray, protested against Henry's regime. Ten days later bills were posted throughout the city and surrounding villages laying out various grievances. This uprising could have been especially dangerous, because by the twenty-seventh of the month up to 9,000 people including some local gentry had gathered at Shipton Moor to demand redress. If they had decided to take up arms, Henry would have had another Shrewsbury on his hands. Though one chronicler said that the leaders, Archbishop Scrope and Mowbray were 'arrayed for battle' that might have been an allegation designed make them appear more guilty.[14]

In the event, the crowd who gathered at Shipton Moor didn't do anything. They just stood and waited, according to Chris Given-Wilson hoping that Northumberland would join them. Ian Mortimer suggests that this event, dubbed the Yorkshire Rising, failed because the rebels had failed to seize Westmorland, but they never seem to have had any definite aim or strategy in mind to begin with.[15] Their procrastination ended when they greeted on 29 May with the arrival of John and Westmorland with heir royal army. Who must have had have heard about what was happening days before and prepared their forces, or they just used the troops they already had with them who had to head off the rebels at Topcliffe not long before. John was just three weeks or so shy of his sixteenth birthday, about the same age his brother was at the Battle of Shrewsbury and was about to face what might be considered his first serious test.

The young John presided over negotiations with the duke of York and Westmorland apparently gave promises that if they were to peacefully disband their forces the king would listen and try to redress their grievances. He lied, although whether he did so knowingly or not is another question. When after many hours, the archbishop and Mowbray ordered their troops to disband, they were immediately arrested and taken to Pontefract Castle in Yorkshire. The incident probably didn't run quite how Shakespeare later portrayed it, with a young John making a charming show of wanting to listen to the potential rebels and happily promising to tell the king of their grievances, before secretly calling in troops to arrest them on charges of treason. The arrest was probably always the intention, but John and Westmorland were likely just relieved to have been able to avoid a pitched battle like last time.

Likely neither John nor Westmorland anticipated how events would pan out for the archbishop. After being taken to Pontefract, the king marched north from Wales, and summoned his council to meet him at Pontefract because he said the earl of Northumberland and other lords had risen up against him. An exaggeration if there ever was one. When he reached Pontefract on 3 June, he actually ordered the steward of his household, Sir John Stanley, to seize and take control of the city of York. Not since the days of William the Conqueror on the cusp of the infamous Harrying of the North had a king of England ridden North with the apparent intent of taking punitive action against his own subjects and England's second city of York. The people of the city were genuinely afraid of what the king might do because they 'streamed out to meet him, 'barefooted and bareheaded, wearing filthy rags, and, carrying swords in their hands [to surrender], they pleaded for pardon, weeping and wailing miserably'. Henry 'rebuked them fiercely' and ordered them back into the city to await his pleasure.[16]

In the meantime, the archbishop of Canterbury, Thomas Arundel, had heard of events in the North and that the king had refused to meet with Richard Scope. He too feared what the king intended and rode swiftly North. The 52-year-old archbishop rode through the night, arriving at York on the morning of 6 June. The very same day, Scrope and his fellows were put on trial and condemned to death. The 'trial' though was something of a farce- one account says that the chief justice walked out in disgust because the assembled lords did not have the authority to condemn an archbishop. Another says that York was tried in the absence of his fellow primate the archbishop of Canterbury when the king feigned concern at his exhaustion and told him to go and have breakfast.[17]

Two days later, on 8 June 1405 Richard Scrope, archbishop of York and the 19-year-old Thomas Mowbray, son and heir of the other Thomas Mowbray, once Henry's friend and fellow appellant, were beheaded by sword outside York, according to tradition in a field of barley near a windmill. No one had ever dared to execute a bishop before, let alone the second highest churchman in the country. It was a shocking act, and one for which Thomas Arundel had already foretold of dire consequences before it even happened. Mowbray's death must also have been shocking he was the son and heir of the former earl of Norfolk, and former appellant who had died in Venice five years earlier. In the fifteenth century, males were usually counted as coming of age at 21 and so a 19-year-old may still have been counted as a boy. A couple of dozen more executions followed, and in July Henry marched to Berwick to set about expelling the recalcitrant earl of Northumberland from his stronghold. Although he escaped into Scotland, Berwick and the Percy stronghold of Alnwick fell into royal hands.

John passed the testing year of 1405 with flying colours when he and Westmorland were able to stamp out two attempted insurrections in Yorkshire within two weeks and significantly without a single loss of life among royalist forces. He'd proved himself highly capable in the duty his father assigned to him, and as a commander when he took the actions needed without having to engage the opposition in a fight. He also underscored his loyalty to his father by writing to the people of the city of York to rebuke them for protests over the death of their archbishop. Even if he didn't support the decision on a personal level, he certainly stood by it politically.

For much of his later life, John would be overshadowed by his more famous older brother, Henry, yet clues to his skill, ingenuity and competence as a leader and soldier can be found throughout his life and career, beginning in his teens. In his capacity as warden of the East March, John was likely at his father's side during the campaign of July 1405 aimed at ousting the earl of Northumberland from power permanently. He remained in the Marches for the next eight years, giving him perhaps more time of military service and experience overall than his brother.

Between 1403 and 1405 John was successively granted more and more land from confiscated Percy estates in the North, at least those which the king was able to get hold of when the earl was still alive. One of those he received was Ogelby in Wiltshire. This would have helped to give him some independent income, along with the few lands he had been granted earlier on in his life. It was expected for the king to provide for his younger sons although he does not seem to have been in any particular hurry to do so. As a result, John was almost always strapped for cash. Almost as soon as his father returned south after the campaign of 1405 things became difficult for him because of financial troubles.

Some £11,450 was raised in the Lords in 1406 and was distributed among John and his two older brothers, who had been placed in charge of the defence of the borders or English territories in Wales, Ireland and Northern England respectively. In 1406, fortune favoured

England when the 11-year-old James, Earl of Carrick was captured off the coast of Yorkshire. Carrick was the heir to the throne of Scotland, and he was making his way to France. The so called 'auld alliance' between France and Scotland which had existed since the thirteenth or fourteenth century still ran strong and Scottish incursions across the border often had French aid or support behind them. Scottish-French marriages were also common. Two weeks later, his father, the king of Scotland died making the young James technically the new king, but now he was a prisoner under English control and an important bargaining chip. The death of the king of Scots left the kingdom basically in the hands of his younger brother, Robert Stewart, Duke of Albany who served as regent. Albany was a controversial figure who was said to have been more interested in serving his own needs than getting his young nephew back or serving the good of the kingdom. Significantly for Henry though, Albany was not bound by any of the alliances which his predecessor had made and at least appeared to be more open to negotiation. Instead of attacking England in the name of the deposed Richard II or in alliance with the Percys, Albany had his own agenda.

In Wales, progress was also being made with a campaign designed to surround Snowdonia. It didn't help that the French troops which had been sent to Pembrokeshire the year before went home without having done very much. In April, the English won a significant victory, killing 1,000 Welsh troops and one of Glyn Dŵr's sons. Although the earl of Northumberland fled to Wales from Scotland where he had been staying after the events of the previous year, he was a fugitive and his ability to raise troops and garner support was rather more limited than it had been before since he had basically been stripped of most of his lands and was so far removed from his centre of power.

In July, parliament passed an act entailing the crown in the male line. This meant that if Prince Henry was to die without an heir, his brother Thomas was to become king, and if Thomas died, it would go to John. John was only a few days shy of his sixteenth birthday when this act was passed, and of course probably assumed that such an event would never happen. Henry was by then 18 and Henry Beaufort, Bishop of Winchester had already been dispatched to France to try and find a bride for him. He was, ironically, angling for one of King Charles VI of France's daughters, possibly even Isabella who had been the wife of Richard II. Nearly six years after the deposition of her husband she would have only been a couple of years younger than her potential groom. Had Prince Henry married Isabella, some fifteen years before he married her sister who knows if things would have turned out differently. He would likely have been succeeded by a teenager instead of a child upon his death. In the event, Bishop Beaufort's negotiations came to nothing: although the French were no longer actively attacking England, they were still reluctant to marry the king's daughter to the son of Henry IV because of his usurpation. Officially they didn't consider Henry to be secure on the throne, but it probably didn't help that England was seeking the hand of the former wife of Richard II for the son of the man who usurped him.

France was also beset with internal problems, with a rivalry between the king's brothers the duke of Orleans and the duke of Burgundy. Although they had been persuaded to temporarily come to terms in the summer of 1406 and when the negotiations for the young prince's marriage broke down, the king even went so far as to write to the people of England telling them to overthrow Henry and restore the 'true' line of the English: presumably a reference to the heirs of Sir Roger Mortimer. During the parliament of 1406, Henry fell ill for the first time, although on this occasion it seems to have been covered up reasonably well and he was fit enough to see off his daughter Philippa, who was married to Eric of Pomerania, heir to the thrones of Denmark, Norway and Sweden. They were married in October, although she left in August 1046, before she was even 12 years of age, with an entourage of various English dignitaries. Philippa and Eric might be familiar to people who have watched the Netflix series, *The King*, loosely based on the events of Shakespeare's *Henry V*. Philippa was marred to Eric for nearly twenty years and although they had no children, she proved to be a very popular ruler in Denmark.

John may not have attended the Lords in person, because of the necessity of his duty in the North. They were greater after 1405 when more royal powers were vested in him (as constable) and as the protector. It didn't help that his mentor Northumberland wasn't interested in earning the loyalty of former Percy retainers and instead preferred to build up his own power base in Yorkshire.

One can feel John's frustration in the correspondence to his father in the years following 1405–06. He wrote to the council many times bemoaning his lack of money. That which he was allocated in 1406 was used up quickly, paying soldiers and maintaining a small army in the North cost money, as did maintaining a household. Especially when John was basically carrying much of the responsibility for the defence of the northern border himself. In 1407, John wrote a series of letters to his father and to the privy council telling them about the poor state of repair of the walls and defences of the city of Berwick. They were falling down in places (much of the damage had been caused by the kings artillery). He worried that this left the city open to attack, and his guess was correct, because Berwick was eventually recaptured.[18]

He also wrote 'in haste' from his base near Warkworth Castle in Northumberland about the castles of Jedburgh and Fast Castle which had been entrusted to him. Here, the garrisons were threatening to desert because they had not been paid and their wages were badly in arrears. The victuals of the garrison were also being stolen during constant Scottish raids. Jedburgh, like Berwick was later taken by the Scots and the captain forced to abandon it whilst still awaiting his troops wages.[19] John did what he could, including melting down some of his plate and pawning jewels to pay some of his troops. His letter is interesting because John had to couch his desperate need for money in terms of protecting and defending the honour of his father who would be shamed by any castles lost to his enemies. By this time, John may have already developed his reputation for steadfast loyalty and dutifulness which has remained with him to this day. It was a reputation which seems to have been well earned. In 1407 John was still only 18 years of age but was going out of the way to try to provide for his soldier's wages and already had years of military and leadership experience in his own right. All of the sons of Henry IV were said to have been tall and physically muscular as adults: Henry was at least 6 foot tall as an adult, and John seems to have been of a similar height.

Despite the apparent lack of financial aid from his father, John did have assistance in bringing hardcore Percy adherents back into the fold, including the knights Sir Thomas and Sir John Grey of Heton and John Creswell. These three were indented to serve John on the borders after the death of the earl of Northumberland in 1408. The once great earl died at the Battle of Bramham Moor in February 1408, a last-ditch attempt to raise a rebellion and sweep King Henry from power. The course and outcome of the battle isn't well recorded, but we know that it was a victory for the royalist forces though none of the royal family were actually there; the royalist army was commanded by Sir Thomas Rokeby the High Sheriff of Yorkshire. After the battle, his head was placed on London Bridge. Percy's heir was his grandson who was about 15 years of age at the time of his death. Although old enough, he was living in exile in Scotland and Henry IV wasn't overly keen on the boy coming back, let alone restoring him to his estates.

With these former Percy adherents, and Northumberland's death, John at least had more support. In 1408–09 some of his predictions of what would happen if resources were not directed towards the protection and defences of some border fortresses came true. Jedbugh and Berwick were taken and in 1408 John once again wrote a letter complaining about the lawless state of the borderlands. He spoke of the 'armed incursions, robberies, pillages, taking of prisoners, cattle raids … and other acts of war' habitually committed in the county. In some cases, it is unclear whether these acts were being committed by Percy loyalists or were part of the pattern of raids which had become normal across the English and Scottish borders. Jedburgh and Berwick had been retaken by the Scots and so had nothing to do with the Percys. In fact, they were largely due to the actions of James Douglas, Earl of Douglas who was the Scottish counterpart of John as warden of the Marches. As early as 1405 he had written to King Henry defending his actions in attacking Berwick and complaining about English outrages in Scotland including the harrying of 'Lauderdale, Cheviot Dale and a part of Catterick Forest.[20] John had sat and presided over various attempted negotiations between the English and the Scots, listening to the delegations from both sides and at one point wrote to his father asking for advice. These negotiations dragged on for more than a year, from 1406–1407 and were pretty much fruitless.

Douglas had returned to raiding the border following a period of captivity in England by 1410–11 and had been behind yet another attack on Berwick (a city which was fought over so many times it was hard to live let alone thrive there) as well as some of the other raids. The English had no doubt returned to these activities for their part was well. The royal response to it was not just to finally pour more resources into the North, but also the beginning of attempt to re-assert law and order by telling itinerant royal justices to go North several times a year, in order that people seeking redress did not have to go all the way to Westminster, although apparently neither Henry IV nor his successor seem to have been especially consistent in ensuring this took place nor enforcing the so-called laws of the March. John's father did help assist the financial strain by handing over all of the remaining Percy and Hotspur lands which were still in royal lands and a proposal was even made that John could marry one of the daughters of the regent of Scotland. At 21 John would have been of an age for marriage even though all of his brothers were still single, but the proposal never came to anything.

Ultimately it was to be efforts at negotiation which made the real difference. In the closing years of Henry IV's reign a series if truces were made in France with the supervision of the duke of Clarence,

Henry's second son. One of these involved extracting a promise for a seven-year cessation of hostilities between the English and Scots was agreed as part of the treaty of Bourges in December 1411. Clarence sent orders to England to make certain that John and Westmorland had the chance to proclaim the terms of the agreement far and wide. It seems to have been largely upheld by both sides, at least for the first few years, meaning that John had one less front to fight on. By 1411 John, now an adult of 22, who had been warden of the East March for eight turbulent years. The North was arguably more of a home to him then his family's centre of power in the Midlands where he grew up had ever been, since he had spent more than a third of his life there. There is evidence that John, then in his twenties did start making some trips to London in the second decade of the 1400s. By then he could attend the Lords or meetings of the council in his own right. One London based chronicle tells us about how fights broke out between in 1410–11 between Londoners and the retainers of John's brother Thomas and on one occasion in 1410 an affray broke out in Eastcheap which involved John's retainers as well.[21]

John was probably starting to go to London more often because his father was beset by ill-health and his presence and ability to conduct business independently was important. Also, from 1411 his brother Thomas was beginning to take a more prominent role in government and later went on an expedition to France. This left something of a power vacuum which John sort of stepped into: he didn't take an active role in government, but he did need to be closer to the centre of government more often rather than patrolling the Marches of the North. Now that the Percy threat had been neutralised and things were sort of settling in Scotland, he could afford to do that. John is noted at this time to have been a young man of good morals, 'dutiful and upright, a man of good habits and a worker for peace'. This is a modern assessment which needs to be taken with perhaps a helping of salt, as the 'worker for peace' part didn't always apply but it seems to be broadly accurate. John wasn't responsible for the brawling of his men in London but had served his father's interests loyally for more than a decade and was trusted to take a leading role in negotiations.

King Henry's illness was an unidentified but serious condition of the skin and nerves which often left him incapacitated, and having to wear gloves when he was able to appear in public. He was afflicted with bouts of illness from 1405 onwards with some of the worst bouts in 1408, 1409 and 1412. His disease hasn't been identified by modern historians, but medieval chroniclers called it leprosy and said that it he was struck down with the illness as a judgement from God for his treatment of Archbishop Richard Scrope.[22] When his illness first struck him, Henry would probably have been glad of his four teenage sons who ably served him and defended his realm but by 1411–12 he was beginning to consider it a mixed blessing. There is no evidence that he had any worries or problems about John, they came from another quarter, his eldest son and heir, Henry. Henry disagreed with his father's stance and policy in France, favouring the duke of Burgundy instead of his father's tendency to favour the duke of Orleans.

During his father's illness, the young prince of Wales wielded power as a virtual regent, and he opposed much of his father's foreign policy. From November 1411, matters came to a head when the younger Henry began openly favouring the duke of Burgundy in defiance of his father. There was even a suggestion that he should marry the daughter of John the Fearless, Duke of Burgundy but it did not come to anything. From this time, Henry was increasingly pushed out of government by his father and his eldest brother, Thomas who had long been their father's favourite. Thomas even led a campaign into France supporting the duke of a Orléans and was given much of the power his brother should have had. This led even to rumours by some chroniclers that King Henry intended to disinherit his eldest son in favour of his more obedient second son. Whether he ever seriously intended to do so was doubtful, but the mere suggestion was enough to create tension.

In 1412, under the terms of a treaty made with the French the duke of Orléans took the radical step of offering to cede control of the Duchy of Aquitaine to Henry IV. The duchy had of course belonged to the kings of England for many generations, since the marriage of Henry II to Eleanor of Aquitaine way back in the twelfth century, but much territory had been lost since then. Clarence, of course, eagerly encouraged his father to accept the offer. However, the condition was that England provide military assistance in Orléans struggle against the duke of Burgundy. Henry IV was in no position to provide that military assistance because of his increasingly fragile health, and his eldest son would not have done so even if ordered to: that only left Clarence. He departed for France in the summer with a force of 4,000 men, and engaged in the age-old tactic of the *chevauchée*, which involved devastating and burning the lands of an enemy combatant. Even though Clarence's expedition achieved very little and ended in him being paid off by the Armagnacs after they came to terms with Burgundy, it did result in some people seeing him as the most warlike of his bothers. This could have caused problems for Henry had Clarence been present at the time of their father's death, but his adventuring in France removed him from the picture until after it happened.

Henry IV died on 20 March 1413 in Westminster. Tradition has it that he died in the Jerusalem Chamber, part of what was then the royal Palace of Westminster but no longer exists. The chamber named after the city sacred to Christianity was the closest that Henry came to dying in Jerusalem, as a prophesy had allegedly said he would. He was only 47 years old: not old even by medieval standards. His body had been wracked by near constant illness for the last several years, and as many historians have asserted the stress and burdens of kingship probably contributed to his death. It is remarkable that a king who usurped the throne as Henry had managed to die peacefully in his bed, and to pass the throne onto his son. However, if Clarence had been in England, it is possible – not necessarily probable but possible – that his eldest son's succession might have been contested.

Wales

Shrewsbury did not end the problem of the conflict with Wales. Glyn Dŵr was of course still alive, and had been able to make a tentative alliance with France. Henry's marriage to Joan of Navarre, the dowager duchess of Brittany had not gone down at all well in France, and he attracted the special ire of Louis, Duke of Orleans, the brother of the king of France. Orleans had intermittently caused problems throughout Henry's reign, including sending an expeditionary force to Scotland and raiding English coastal ports.

Glyn Dŵr's even entered a treaty with Charles VI of France himself, wanting to sweep away the Lancastrian usurper. The Welsh Lord's actions and the amount of success he had appear to testify to how unpopular Henry IV's regime was in the early years of his reign. Louis, Duke of Orleans had once been a close friend and associate of Henry but felt betrayed by his actions in 1399 and the deposition of Richard and he felt offended by England's courting of his great rival the duke of Burgundy.

The king of France had not forgotten how Henry sent his daughter Isabella back (minus some of her jewellery) and instability in England was always something worth exploiting. The French king authorised the count of La Marche to take a thousand men at arms and crossbowmen to Pembroke to fight in the aid of Glyn Dŵr in 1404.

It was in July that same year that the young Prince Henry returned to his office as lieutenant of Wales after nearly a year of convalescence from his injuries sustained at Shrewsbury: and his return turned the tide of the war. English policy had been defensive for the last year consisting of a near constant round of recapturing or reliving cities or castles under siege. After the young prince returned to the frontlines, and more money was poured into his war effort, there was more success.

Another large expeditionary force of French troops was dispatched to Pembroke again in 1405, but they achieved little except taking

Carmarthen and even that was taken by negotiation rather than siege. Within a few weeks of arrival, most of the French forces returned home. Although Glyn Dŵr retained hopes of a future Franco-Welsh alliance, 1405 marked a turning point when the English became more actively aggressive in policy towards those who had previously been the enemies and rivals of Henry. France began to distance itself from Wales, and pursuing other alliances and increasingly beset by instability in the ranks of its own nobles.

The so called 'Pirate War' consisting of piracy in the Channel and raids on English coastal towns wound down, and, instead, England began making sorties onto the French coast, with Thomas the second son of the king even being sent to command some of the ships. It was a reversal of the events of two years before. A truce between France and England had been renewed two years earlier, and the French had consistently ignored. In the years before 1405 Henry's 'empire' seemed poised to collapse. This consisted of Wales, Ireland and the parts of France still held by the English monarchy, but afterwards, the ousting of Northumberland and the crushing of his rebellions in the North, as well as the capture of the young heir to throne of Scotland brought an end of most of the turbulence in the North, and England's newly aggressive policy in the Channel helped protect English shipping by retaliating in kind and occasionally intercepting the pirate vessels.

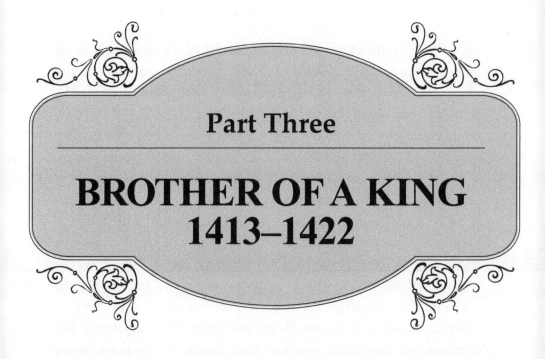

Part Three

BROTHER OF A KING
1413–1422

Chapter Four

A New King

Henry, the eldest son of King Henry IV was crowned king at the age of 26 in April 1413. His coronation was marked with a snowstorm. The unseasonable weather was interpreted by some as a bad omen, but not by the king himself. Henry V is a king who invokes strong feelings in many people to this day: he is often either loved and admired as one of the great medieval warrior-kings; a paragon of the chivalric ideals or denounced as a brutal tyrant and religious fanatic. Malcolm Vale and others have revealed that there was a lot more to Henry than just the warlord who achieved victory at Agincourt, but this is not a biography of Henry. It may be interesting to note that one of Henry's earliest acts as king, however, was something which strikes modern readers and unexpected: he commissioned an effigy to be placed on the tomb of his mother, Mary de Bohun at Leicester. Henry and his brothers apparently still remembered the mother who had died almost twenty years before with fondness and wanted to honour her memory.

It might strike us as remarkable that the famous (or infamous) fifteenth-century warrior-king engaged in such a sentimental act, but Henry was a man of contradictions who took after his mother in more ways that are apparent today. It is also interesting to note that her son had to perform this act since his father evidently made no attempt to do so. Perhaps he thought it was inappropriate after he remarried. Henry also had the remains of Richard II moved and reburied with due ceremony in Westminster Abbey. This act marked the policy Henry would adopt in the early part of his reign: to reconcile and bring back into the fold those who had been disinherited or branded as traitors during his father's reign. Much of his first Parliament which was held in May 1413 was devoted to wrapping up business in his father's reign and matters relating to law and order, including miscarriages of justice and dealing with abuses and corruption by judges. Little was done on the political side of things. Although the matters the Lords did deal with were part of the everyday minutia of government which the king had to have a head for.

In the previous chapters, it was shown that Henry and his brothers were interested in reading. Henry had a special desk designed with two tiers to store his books in. This was apparently housed in his chambers at Eltham Palace, where he stayed frequently. Henry owned a very early copy of Chaucer's *Troilus and Criseyde* or *Troilus and Cressida:* a chivalric romance with shades of Romeo and Juliet set in ancient Troy. The book was especially made for Henry and had designs and images tailored to his tastes. Considering his family's association with Chaucer, it's not a surprise that Henry had one of his books. He later commissioned John Lydgate, a well-known monk and poet to create a book on the history of Troy for him,

It was not until the following session and second parliament of his reign in May 1414 that Henry promoted his younger brothers, raising them to the higher nobility by making all of them royal dukes. John was made duke of Bedford and Humphrey was made duke of Gloucester. They were also both given additional titles as earls. John was earl of Kendal, and Humphrey was earl of Pembroke. Earl of Kendal was a good fit for John, who had been Warden of the East March and operated in the North for so long. Although the formal appointment ended in 1414, John still found himself often entrusted with patrolling and protecting the borders of his brother's realm.

Henry also brought Edmund and Roger Mortimer – the sons of the man who had once been the nominated heirs to Richard II – back into the fold. They had been living in a virtual state of captivity for much of their lives, and now were brought to court and restored them many of their lands and titles. Henry also restored the duke of York 'him to his estate, name, repute and honour' and declared him to be a 'a good and loyal liege to his father, formerly king, as well as to himself'.[1] This was Edward of Norwich, the eldest son of Edmund of Langley who had been duke of York during Richard II's reign. York had a rather chequered relationship with Henry IV. After his involvement with the Epiphany Rising as a young man, he had reportedly been involved in another plot against King Henry. Although the real instigator of that plan was his younger sister, Constance, it is unclear to what extent Edward was truly involved. York also seems to have at one point, harboured romantic feelings for Queen Joan; feelings which landed him in trouble. He wrote letters to the queen. Of course, for another man to make any kind of romantic gesture towards the wife of a king was considered a treasonable act, but the late King Henry didn't punish him too severely, suggesting he took it as a harmless infatuation.[2] He was never stripped of all his lands or estates, although he did temporarily lose some. York was more concerned though about how events of the past had left him with a dubious reputation: hence the references to his 'name and honour'.

In 1414, Edward of York renounced one of his lesser titles, that the of the earl of Cambridge. The title was then bestowed upon his younger brother, Richard, a man who would come to prominence for the wrong reasons in the following year. It is interesting that what Henry gave to York on the one hand he was encouraged to delegate and give away on the other Perhaps the king did not want his cousin to hold too much land and prominence, or the move was made by Edward himself to recognise his brother's status as heir apparent to the dukedom since he was childless.

At 24 John was of an age when most nobles (especially those of the royal blood) would have been married. John was not, nor were any of his other brothers, with the notable exception of Thomas, Duke of Clarence. Clarence had married one Margaret Holland in 1410: the marriage was rather controversial since she was in fact the widow of his own uncle, John Beaufort, Duke of Somerset.[3] This John Beaufort was one of the original four Beaufort siblings: three boys and one girl who were the half-siblings of King Henry IV. Thomas appears to have married the woman who had been his aunt by marriage for the money and land which she bought him: some £1,400 per year and the custody his uncle's underage heirs as well as their inheritance. Although she wàs only about 22 years of age, she had already bore several children to her first husband, but she was still considered young enough to potentially have more. Unfortunately for Thomas, she didn't.

At some point during his brother's reign, John became involved with a woman whose name and identity have sadly been lost to history. This was probably the time in John's life when he had most opportunity to associate with women, whether at court or in the household of one of his peers. As Warden of the East March, he probably had very little opportunity to meet any women close to his age, let alone suitable marriage material (although there were some marriage proposals which fell through), apart from perhaps Ralph Neville's daughters. Most of whom were much younger than him anyway and were also his first cousins through their mother Joan Beaufort. Marriage to cousins wasn't unusual but it seems Henry IV wanted rather more advantageous and prestigious matches for his sons.

It is likely that that his mistress was of much lower rank to him, and a sad fact of history that unless the mistresses of noblemen played some major role in events, or their liaisons were openly acknowledged the names of these women went unrecorded. All we know of John's mistress is that she bore him two children named Mary and Richard. Even their exact dates of birth are unknown since they were not legitimate children and so were not potential heirs to the throne. All we know is that they were born at some point during Henry V's nine-year reign, since they appear in the records from their teens onwards. Mary and Richard were to be the only surviving children that John would ever have, and it is a shame that so much of their lives were poorly recorded. It is one of the many contradictions of this time that a person could be considered to be pious and morally upright despite having several children out of wedlock.

In the medieval period, pre-marital sex was not considered irreconcilable with holding strong religious beliefs or personal ethics largely because attitudes towards sex were different then. For a young man like John, it was almost expected to have liaisons before (and outside of) marriage. He may well have had a long term and even a monogamous relationship with the mother of his children. He certainly acknowledged and provided for his children by the unknown lady. Few medieval nobleman took the radical step which his grandfather had of marrying a mistress – and Katherine Swynford wasn't from the lowest order. She had been a lady in waiting to a queen and was the widow of a knight. Possibly John's mistress was a servant or a commoner whom he felt he could not marry because she was of much lower social rank and station than him and such a match would not have been considered appropriate.

Now the duke of Bedford, John's brother began to entrust him with more responsibilities. He seems to have continued in his work as Warden of the East March until 1414 but afterwards John would experience several periods in which he was the protector and regent of the realm. That he or Humphrey Duke of Gloucester were chosen for this role instead of Thomas of Clarence tells us something about the still troubled relationship the new king had with the brother who was nearest to him in age.

In the opening months of 1414, all royal plans were put on hold by an unexpected event known as the Oldcastle Rising or the Lollard Rising. It was instigated by Sir John Oldcastle and included a group of Christian nonconformists known as the Lollards who traced their origins to the writings and teachings of the priest, theologian and reformer John Wycliffe. They are often considered to be 'proto-Protestants' because some of their beliefs had a lot in common with the later Protestants. John Wycliffe died in the 1380s and by 1413 a lot of Lollards had diverged from his original teachings and intent. Wycliffe himself was mostly focused on theological concerns such as the doctrine of transubstantiation and tended to keep out of politics: although he did not believe that the church should possess great wealth, he was always careful not to put any politically incendiary ideas into action. Before Wycliffe, England had not had its own home-grown 'heretical' movement and initially many did not know how to respond to Wycliffe and his adherents.

The Lollards, as they came to be known, did undergo persecution under Richard II and this worsened under Henry IV. Ironically, Henry's father had once been one of Wycliffe's most erstwhile supporters who passed the first-ever law in England allowing for the burning of heretics. The process by which a person was condemned for heresy was convoluted. Primarily, it was under the remit of the church and heretics were tried independently of any secular or civil court. However, the church could not impose the penalty of death without the approval of secular authorities and had to turn a convicted person over to those secular authorities for punishment. This will become significant later in this study with the more famous case of a French peasant girl named Joan of Arc.

The Oldcastle Rising

In the closing months of 1413, an alleged plot was hatched to overthrow the government. This plot was spearheaded by one Sir John Oldcastle, a long-time Lancastrian retainer who had been a friend of Prince Henry and had served in Wales. Oldcastle's Lollard sympathies were well known to the point that he may have become 'the most prominent heretical layman in the country'[4]. After the death of Henry IV who had tolerated his activities, the archbishop of Canterbury began proceedings against Oldcastle but had to tread carefully thanks to his friendship with the new king. Remarkably, the archbishop was to condemn Oldcastle for heresy in a church court, despite the king trying to intervene: an action which reveals that the church was not beholden to the state when it came to trying people for crimes which hinged on theological and religious concerns, proving it had a great measure of independence.

Contrary to modern ideas, the medieval church did not go around burning people for heresy left, right and centre: even after Oldcastle was condemned by the archbishop, he was given forty days in which to recant. Although, had he been a commoner and not had a connection with the king, this might not have happened. He was committed to the Tower of London to give him time to recant his beliefs which proved to be a bad idea, because by 19 October he escaped from the Tower with the aid of friends in the capital, and was able to rally Lollards and other supporters from across the country. They arranged to gather together at St Giles Fields outside London on the night of 9 January 1414 with the alleged intent to try to kidnap the king and his brothers and take control of the government.

Once again, the Lancastrian network of intelligence won. Henry learned of the plot through informers and spies, and likely someone who betrayed the revolt, and there are records of payments to informants among the yeomanry (landed peasants or commoners). So, the king was ready when the would-be rebels arrived at St Giles Fields outside London on the night of the 9/10 January. He gathered troops at nearby Clerkenwell, and they charged before those gathered could reach the main camp. Oldcastle himself fled at the first sight of the king's troops leaving his compatriots to their mercy.

The aftermath of the so-called 'Oldcastle Rising' proved to be one of the most controversial of Henry's reign. Not in the sight of contemporaries but certainly to modern historians. Forty people who had taken part in the rebellion were executed as rebels and seven were burned for heresy. Modern historians have tended to interpret the seven burnings as evidence of Henry's religious extremism and bigotry, but as Malcolm Vale pointed out, this event was in the context of an attempted insurrection and many other European rulers were far harsher at cracking down on supposed 'heresy' than Henry, having dozens or hundreds punished. It is also worth noting that some historians have noticed that Henry was never the 'instigator of events' when it came to the persecution of Lollards or the punishment of heretics.[5] Even the Oldcastle Rising was largely the result of the archbishop of Canterbury being rather too zealous in his pursuit of his aims: the king only got involved when it involved a threat to his own life or safety. The numbers accused of rebellion in the aftermath of the Oldcastle Rising suggest the vast majority of those who appeared that January night was not motivated by religious devotion but perhaps by political or personal concerns. As we've also already seen, the archbishop of Canterbury was an especially ardent heretic hunter, and the Oldcastle Rising might have only served to vindicate the fears he had stoked in the minds of many of the ruling elites. Oldcastle went on the run after the failed rising and kept hidden for nearly four years.

After the blip of the Oldcastle Rising, Henry put much of his time and effort into matters relating to France. For the first two years of his reign he became somewhat preoccupied with regaining his ancestral lands in France. It should be noted though that at this point there is no specific evidence that Henry wanted or intended to claim the throne of France. That only came later. Neither was going to war his first resort: from the time of his first time president over the Great Council in June 1413 until the following year he concentrated most of his energies on said diplomatic negotiations. In 1414, Henry made the unusual move of summoning the Lords twice: the first time in April as mentioned was when he conveyed dukedoms on his younger brothers, but the second time in November was more focused on gaining noble backing (and money) to prop up his efforts in France.

It is worth noting that before 1413, France was in a state of near civil war. During King Charles VI bouts of madness, much of his power had been held by his younger brother Louis I, coronation of Orléans but was challenged by their cousin Phillip the Bold, coronation of Burgundy, and then by his son, John the Fearless for the regency and custody of Charles VI's children and heirs to the throne. In the opening years of the fifteenth century, their rivalries led to a rather farcical situation in which the dauphin of France was kidnapped various times by both parties. Louis of Orléans became a controversial figure due not only to the amount of land and political power he wielded, but also for his relationship with King Charles' wife and his sister- in- law, Isabeau of Bavaria. They became so close there were rumours Louis was involved in an incestuous relationship with her and that he was the father of one of her children. This came to a head in 1407 when he was brutally murdered on the streets of Paris on the orders of his cousin, John I, Duke of Burgundy with whom he had a long-running political and personal dispute. John wasn't even quiet about having killed the king's own brother: he openly admitted to his involvement and even tried to have the act officially justified. The murder transformed in an instant what had been a political crisis in France into a bitter feud between members of the royal family, which resembled England's later Wars of the Roses. Burgundy's probable murder of his relative backfired when he replaced one adversary with another: Louis' son, Charles proved to be an especially formidable opponent who would never allow what had happened to his father to be forgotten.

Both parties in France sought and courted foreign backing at various times, Henry V was able to exploit this internal division in France to his own advantage. It has been mentioned that he favoured the party of the duke of Burgundy and consistently sought an alliance with John the Fearless. In early 1414, John was effectively out of Paris after a failed attempt to take control of the city at the head of an army and take control of the dauphin. The people closed the gates against him, and he was forced to withdraw ignominiously back to his own lands. Charles, the duke of Orléans (since his father's murder seven years earlier) and his allies formally declared war on Burgundy with the official backing of the king and the dauphin. In this situation, it is no wonder Burgundy was so willing to run into the arms of the English and the receptive Henry V.

Henry, however, was playing a cunning game of negotiating with the duke of Burgundy and the Armagnac faction at the same time, but using separate ambassadors. By exploiting the divisions, he intended that Burgundy would provide backing for (or at least not openly oppose) any potential invasion of France but at the same time give the Armagnacs the impression he intended to seriously sue for peace. At one point, Henry's ambassadors were simultaneously negotiating for him to marry Katherine, daughter of the king of France and making similar arrangements to marry the daughter of the duke of Burgundy, also called Catherine. Henry's negotiations with Burgundy were not wholly self-centred though: he ruled parts of the county of Flanders which had been an important trading partner with England for many years, but it certainly put him in a stronger position to negotiate with France. In April 1414 at least (the time of his first Parliament that year when he created his brothers dukes), the Commons didn't prove to be quite so keen on declaring war as their king was and encouraged him to continue with negotiations. This he did, but with a rather more hostile edge.

Henry had given his ambassadors authority to take the homage of the duke of Burgundy. Taking homage was a big deal; it essentially meant swearing allegiance and fealty to a lord usually in return for certain lands. It looks like Henry was hoping that Burgundy might be willing to do this to him, as the kings of England had once been forced to ritually swear homage to the kings of France for their lands there. This was too ambitious, even for Henry. Even if Burgundy was willing to turn a blind eye to an invasion of France, he wasn't prepared to countenance reneging on his homage to the king of France: and besides for much of 1414 and through into the next year he was occupied fighting off his domestic adversaries.

In King Henry's letters to Charles, he begins referring to him as 'our adversary' and adopting an increasingly belligerent tone. This resulted from his territorial demands not being met, as he expected them not to. Henry wanted the old lands of Aquitaine, Anjou, and Normandy but also several lands which had been outside the old possessions of the kings of England including parts of Brittany and Flanders the lordship of Provence as well as 1.6 million crowns for a dowry when he married the king of France's daughter. The demands were, of course, outrageous and the French would never agree to such terms. The idea was that they would be haggled down to something more reasonable, a process which continued until early 1415 when after many rounds of backing and forthing, the French offered Henry two-thirds of the Duchy of Aquitaine (minus his other territorial demands) and 800,000 crowns as a dowry, which was not accepted.

It is unlikely that Henry ever seriously wanted peace with France. Within days of the final set of ambassadors returning to France, Henry was already informing the mayor and aldermen of London that he planned to cross the Channel and invade France. For months before, he had been building up his own personal invasion fleet, consisting of ships he had built and various foreign vessels which had been captured and reworked. He also commissioned a servant and clerk to gather staff to man his new ships, which implies a fifteenth-century form of a pressgang. Henry called parliament for April 1414, and on that occasion (unlike a year before) they approved his desire to go to war with France, and he began to officially make plans for invasion.

Meanwhile, Henry confirmed his brother in the position of warden of the West March at the start of his reign. Although he was now duke of Bedford, he still had important duties in the North and was still accompanied by the earl of Westmorland. Henry made it his business to repair and rebuild some of the castles on the Scottish border which had been damaged in the raids of the preceding years and this was what John spent the first year or so of his brother's reign doing before being created duke of Bedford and brought into his brother's inner circle.

In the opening weeks of Henry's reign, the sceptre of Richard II had come back to haunt Henry in the form of handbills being circulated proclaiming that Richard II was still alive and living in Scotland. It was circulated by a man named John Whitelock who had been a former member of Richard's household. It was this act which resulted in Henry's reburial of Richard in Westminster Abbey, but it did not make the threat go away entirely: the fact that the instigator had known Richard might have lent some credibility to his story: and he then escaped from custody to never be recaptured. In 1414, Henry made a treaty with Scotland, and during the second Parliament of that year – he made an agreement to allow the grandson and heir of Henry Percy (also called Henry Percy) to return to England.

John might have been at the castle of Kenilworth, the place of his birth, when in late 1414 or early 1415, Henry played host to a notorious event there. The dauphin of France sent Henry an insulting gift of gaming balls to mock his ambitions in France. Many historians question whether this event ever really took place. The heir to the French throne named Louis was only 17 years old at that time, and France was embroiled in a state of civil war. He had more important things to do than worry about insulting the king of England. The story may have grown out of an event recorded by two contemporary English observers, one of whom, John Strecche, was a canon at the Abbey of the Virgin Mary in Kenilworth. His proximity to Kenilworth could have meant he was even an eyewitness. In his version, there was no 'gift' of balls to Henry. What happened instead was that French ambassadors who had been received at Kenilworth mockingly said they would send the king balls to play with and cushions to sit on: basically, saying that he was too soft and coddled to be a serious threat,[6] upon which the king responded with dry wit: 'If God so wills and my life lasts, I will within a few months play such a game of ball in the Frenchmen's streets, that they shall lose their jest and gain but grief for their game. If they sleep too long upon their cushions in their chamber, perchance before they wish it, I will rouse them from their slumbers by hammering on their doors at dawn.'[7]

This seems more credible than the story of the gaming balls from the dauphin and suggests how Henry's ambitions might have been taken. Kenilworth was one of Henry's favourite residences where he went as often as he could with his brothers and other trusted courtiers. Henry constructed a *pleasance*, or a pleasure garden at Kenilworth. He called it *Le Pleasauntz en Marys*, or the pleasure garden the marsh because the area had once been swampland. He also constructed a large timber banqueting hall surrounded by a wall in the garden where the king could entertain a few select visitors, friends or relatives.[8] Kenilworth was thus supposed to be an escape from court life for Henry (and presumably for his brothers when they went there), and his country retreat. It also gives us glimpses of the more personal and human side of Henry and his brothers who are more often remembered for their military endeavours and campaigns: he enjoyed spending time in a garden and in the company of friends where he could pursue his hobbies and interests.

At the same time, an agreement was also made to release Murdoch, Earl of Fife, the son of the duke of Albany, who had been a prisoner in England since 1402. Henry intended the release of Murdoch and reconciliation with Percy to be part of a wider agreement not only with Scotland but as a means of trying to repair matters between the Nevilles and Percys. In May 1415, only a month after Henry finally received official sanction in the Lords to go to war in France, Murdoch was released from the Tower of London where he had been ensconced for nearly two years. He was supposed to be taken north and exchanged for the young Henry Percy. En route, he was kidnapped by a rogue Lollard knight by the name of Sir Thomas Talbot. He was retrieved a week later and restored to the custody of Ralph Neville.

The missing week, though, proved a problem for Henry, meaning that his exchange of hostages had to be postponed and his agreement with Scotland was not kept. Although John was ever loyal, he may have privately breathed a sigh of relief at this. Although the young Henry Percy was not of age, it would not be long before he reached his majority and sought to reclaim his ancestral lands. John himself held many of them which he had been granted by his father in return for his service and wasn't too keen on relinquishing what he had strived so hard to gain.

The French had ambassadors in England at the same time, and the failed hostage exchange became a perfect pretext for the Scots to attack England once again, which happened in July and was, fortunately for Henry seen off by the knight Sir Robert Umfraville. John was, probably for the first time in more than a decade, not involved in the efforts to repel the Scottish invasion of 1415 because he had resigned his office as Warden of the East March in late 1414 after being appointed duke of Bedford. However, it took time for his replacement to be appointed and to arrive in the North to take up his position: possibly several months. That replacement was actually Edward of Norwich, Duke of York. He was a good choice since he had extensive lands in the North, but he seems to have been treated as a stopgap until Henry Percy could be restored.

When he returned to court John found his brother's preparations for war were in full swing and he was planning to embark in late July, leaving John in charge of England as lieutenant and take Thomas, Duke of Clarence with him to France. Henry already trusted his younger brother with this great responsibility, though John was not the only one of his brothers who would serve in the capacity of a virtual regent. He could not be everywhere at once, so had to swap one position for another, although he would oversee the defence of the entire realm during his brother's absence.

Southampton Plot

In the summer of 1415, trouble was brewing in more than one part of England: the kidnap of a Scottish nobleman by a Lollard dissenter was embarrassing and diplomatically inconvenient. In another part of the kingdom, however, a plot against the king himself was being devised which appeared to sew together all the disparate threads of dissent within the kingdom. We know about this event, known as the Southampton Plot from the confessions of the plotters, extracted after the plot was revealed in late July. The mastermind of the plot, which was supposed to involve an invasion of England from several quarters and placing the young Edmund Mortimer on the throne, was Richard, Earl of Cambridge. He was the younger brother of the duke of York and had only been raised to the higher peerage in the the Lords of April 1414. Officially the second son of Edmund of Langley, Duke of York, Richard had been unusually left nothing in his father's will and indeed was never even mentioned. Modern historians have speculated that he was, in fact, the product of an affair between Isabella of York – the Spanish-born wife of Edmund of Langley and John Holland the half-brother of Richard II and later duke of Exeter. Within a year of rumours allege John had a romantic entanglement with Richard's mother, he seduced and later married Elizabeth, Henry IV's younger sister. She had been betrothed to another man but had a shotgun wedding to John when it was discovered she had become pregnant by him.

Cambridge's career before 1414 was unremarkable. He was then a mere knight and spent some time on the Welsh Borders during Henry IV's reign, and he might have taken part in the duke of Clarence's invasion of France in 1412–13. Cambridge's significance mostly lies in what happened in 1415 and his offspring: he was the father of Richard, Duke of York and the paternal grandfather of both the Yorkist kings. He married Anne, the older sister of Edmund Mortimer. Edmund Mortimer and his brother Roger had been considered the true heirs of Richard II for many years, and there had been a plot involving him when he was a child more than ten years before Henry was seeking to embark on the Agincourt campaign. In February 1405, Constance, Lady Despenser, the younger sister of Richard and Edward, Duke of York, formulated a plan to smuggle the young Edmund Mortimer and his brother Roger to Wales where they could join Glyn Dŵr and their paternal uncle. She bribed a locksmith to make duplicate keys, and managed to get the boys as far as Gloucestershire before they were recaptured. When Constance was brought before the Council to answer for what had happened, she alleged that her brother Edward, Duke of York was, in fact, the real mastermind and that he had also planned to assassinate the king.[9] Why did Constance wish to incriminate her own brother? It is possible that she blamed him for the death of her husband Thomas Despenser who had been lynched following the Epiphany Rising some five years earlier leaving her a widow with three young children and pregnant with her fourth. Edward confessed that he had known about the plot, but only to warn the king and although he was imprisoned for nearly a year and had some of his lands confiscated, he was eventually pardoned. Constance was also imprisoned but was released without charge the following year.

York did not get some of the lands confiscated in 1405 back until 1414, and there appears to have been a permanent rift between him and his sister which was never healed or mended. Although her plans in 1405 came to nothing, it seems a little too much of a coincidence that Constance's younger brother went on to marry the sister of the Mortimer boys a year or two later. She had no cause for animosity with Richard and still probably harboured enough hatred for the Lancastrians to work behind the scenes. We cannot entirely rule out the possibility that Constance might have, therefore, arranged the marriage between Richard and Anne Mortimer, who was only about 15 or 16 at the time. Tradition has it that their marriage was unexpected, rushed and possibly conducted in secret without the consent of Anne's mother and stepfather or the knowledge of the king.

In 1415, therefore, Cambridge, therefore had a strong and a well-known connection with the Mortimers. It is almost unsurprising that he cooked up a plot which involved them, except that he had never shown any treasonable tendencies beforehand and had ostensibly remained loyal to the Lancastrian regime. Nor had Constance's actions a decade earlier particularly helped the lot of Edmund and his brother. Before that, they had been living with the younger royal children in Windsor; afterwards, they were virtual prisoners. Henry V had taken great pains to bring them back into the fold and Edmund was allowed to inherit his family's estates as well as the title of earl of March. Yet for some reason, by the summer of 1415 both Cambridge and Edmund Mortimer had become disaffected enough to start plotting against the Lancastrians. It is unlikely that he had been planning something ever since his marriage to Anne in 1406 or 1408, but something obviously turned him. On Cambridge's part, the cause of his disaffection might have been that despite being raised to the higher nobility and granted the rank of earl, he had not been given any lands which were essential to funding and supporting the lifestyle and expectations which went along with that rank. For Mortimer, the huge fine that Henry imposed for his authorised marriage to a rich heiress might have swayed him.

As Cambridge formulated plans over the summer, he drew others into them in a sort of familial alliance of Northern lords who planned to tap into existing undercurrents of dissent to sweep away the king and his brothers and put Mortimer on the throne. Also involved were Sir Thomas Grey, whose son was betrothed to Cambridge's daughter, and Henry Scrope of Masham. He was a nephew of Archbishop Scrope who had been executed in 1405. At one point, Cambridge told the other conspirators that Murdoch, Earl of Fife was in his possession: suggesting that he was in on the plot to kidnap the Scottish lord, if not actually behind it. He also planned to take Mortimer into Wales to have him crowned and perhaps gather more forces there, along with obtaining the pretender from Scotland. The plot was audacious and complex: probably too complex. Too much hinged on chance and other variables, and people getting involved who had not been consulted, nevertheless, the main ringleaders remained in communication throughout June and July of 1415 until the mustering for war formally began and all were expected to gather at Southampton.

Henry was not wholly ignorant of what was going on. We have already established that he had an extensive network of spies, and they sniffed out that there was a possible conspiracy, they just didn't know the specific details or who was involved: that was until the night of the thirty-first of July. Only days before Henry was due to embark for France and the plotters were intending to put their plan into action. Edmund Mortimer rode to Portchester Castle where the king was staying and revealed the details of the plot to him, betraying his fellow conspirators to almost certain death in the process. The other conspirators were arrested that very night and imprisoned in Southampton Castle (which no longer exists). Detailed confessions were extracted from them although not under torture as that was not the typical legal procedure in England was frowned upon: it is from these confessions that we have a detailed account of the plot and the conspirators' intents.

Henry acted quickly and decisively. Sir Thomas Grey as a mere knight was executed on 2 August only two days after the plot was revealed. Scrope and Cambridge however appealed to their right to be tried before their peers which might have been a stalling tactic with their intention being a trial before the House of Lords when they were due to reconvene in November. If that was what they intended, they were soon disabused of the notion: most of the nobility had gathered at Southampton for the Muster and so a court was soon convened by them presided over by either John, Duke of Bedford or Thomas, Duke of Clarence. Edmund Mortimer was also placed on the commission that tried them, perhaps as a test of his loyalty. The conspirators were, of course, found guilty and executed. It was almost inevitable, although there is some doubt as the legality of Scrope's conviction since all he confessed to was misprision which meant knowing about treason but not disclosing it. Misprision wasn't a capital offence and Edward, the duke of York (who was excluded from the proceedings) had been pardoned for just such a thing. However, Sir Thomas Grey's confession had incriminated him, Cambridge and even others to such an extent that it may have made people believe he was more guilty than he was. There was also a personal element in what was done to Scrope, who was drawn (or dragged) to the place of execution and then hanged as opposed to just being beheaded. He was a Knight of the Garter and had been a close personal friend of Henry V who had acted as an ambassador for several years. Henry may have felt personally betrayed by him and wished to make an example of him. Either way, it is likely that Henry overstepped the law with Scrope's execution.

The Southampton Plot set back Henry's plans for embarkation by two weeks or more, which doesn't sound like much, but it showed Henry that there were people prepared to oppose him and that they could command support among the marginalised and disaffected. This did not put off Henry from his goal: he had eliminated the immediate threat by executing the ringleaders and sailed for France on the tenth of August leaving England in the capable hands of his brother who remained in London in and around Westminster. Henry took their brother the duke of Gloucester with him, and he also took a small company of surgeons. These surgeons were led by Thomas Morstede, the king's own personal surgeon and his colleague William Bradwardyne. Morstede was the replacement for John Bradmore who retired in 1411 and had died the following year. Henry also took also took a band of minstrels with him on the Agincourt campaign. He contracted a man by the name of John Cliffe and seventeen companions for the term of one year and even put down jewels as collateral for their wages.[10]

Chapter Five

Bedford, A Regency and Agincourt

Bedford's first term in office as Lieutenant of England or guardian of England which was the term he used in official documents, was 'not too strenuous'. He had mostly fulfilled his role fitting out and provisioning the king's soldiers and ships and was able to preside over the country in peace for several months. His business was routine as can be shown by the entries in records which he signed off. Dealing with land grants, property disputes, and paying for goods. At one point, he had to order the sheriff of Norfolk to ensure that the men tasked with protecting and guarding the coastline were doing their jobs. This is an interesting case as the entry in the close rolls suggests he was seeing to coastal defences when the king was abroad. Norfolk was the location of the important port towns of Great Yarmouth and more importantly King's Lynn; the latter was England's most important trading hub with the Continent and the Hanseatic League.[1] Bedford also had to write on 18 October a strongly worded order to the mayor of King's Lynn (then known as Bishop's Lynn) to take up his office in person without protests because 'discord and debate has arisen among the burgesses and good men of the town touching the election of a mayor for the coming year, and it is feared are like to continue, to breach of the peace and disturbance of the people' and the king (as well as his brother) 'will is to cherish peace and quiet in all the realm'.[2] To do this, John remarked, he had to trust in the loyalty of his servants and officials.

Henry seems to have been corresponding with his brother from France on a regular basis, but news was taking its time to get through and most of the orders which John issued in the close rolls were probably things which his brother had alerted him to before he left, or which royal servants alerted him to during his brother's absence. One other thing he considered enough of a problem to issue orders about serves as a chilling reminder of the realities of medieval warfare. Several orders from October and November 1415 exist in the close rolls ordering merchants and traders not to sell food to the French or send supplies to anywhere except Calais. Henry was actively laying siege to the town of Harfleur in August, and it would have been considered counter-productive for anyone to sell food to the besieged town, allowing it to hold out for even longer. Even after the siege of Harfleur ended, the king and his servants were still concerned about the routine trade of goods and supplies across the Channel and were keen to redirect it to the English army.[3] John would have heard about the remarkable English victory at Agincourt on 24 October probably before the month ended and was undoubtedly relieved that his beloved brothers (Humphrey, Duke of Gloucester was also on the campaign) had not only survived but had routed the French army.

This book does not focus on the Battle of Agincourt in any detail because John of Bedford was not there, but it did have an impact on his life. He lost his cousin, Edward, Duke of York at the battle, and had it gone differently could have lost one or more of his brothers. At the same battle Charles, Duke of Orléans was captured: he was the son of Duke Louis who had been murdered in 1407 and was to spend nearly twenty-four years in England and not be released until 1440. Although Charles had brothers, his capture effectively neutralised the Armagnac cause for several years. The duke of Burgundy did not bother to even turn up to the battle, although two of his brothers did and both were killed.

Henry did not hurry back to England. It took him until mid-November to return, via Calais, on 4 November John had to preside over a session of the Lords. He had originally planned to hold it in August, but it had to be prorogued or delayed until November: prorogation of the Lords is nothing new. Its business was mostly focused on grants of taxation this time in the form of a subsidy on imports of wool and wine and confirming the sentences on the conspirators behind the Southampton Plot from three months earlier. This was needed because they had not been tried before all the peers of the realm, but they all affirmed by the Lords Spiritual and Temporal. The conquering hero Henry finally embarked for England on the sixteenth of November and returned to praise and celebration – most of it probably arranged by his brother. When he arrived, he found the streets back to London lined with cheering crowds and the same occurred when he went on a circuit around the country to visit various pilgrimage sites including Canterbury Abbey and St Augustine's Priory in the same city, where the Black Prince and victor of Crécy and Poitiers was buried. In London, after the impromptu celebrations by the townspeople after the first news of the victory of Agincourt had broken there were jousts, processions, plays, the ringing of church bells, and reportedly wine instead of water running in some of the city fountains.[4] A special song was also created to mark the king's victory known as the Agincourt Hymn or the Agincourt Carol attributing Henry's victory to the almighty. The author is unknown, but it was designed to be sung in the polyphonic style popular at the time (Polyphony refers to a musical score which is written with two or more melodic lines or sung with two or more tones.) Although the king also knew about and even composed musical scores in this style, it is unlikely the Agincourt Carol was created by Henry himself or a member of his royal chapel but could have instead been made up by soldiers on the campaign or by someone in England who had heard an account of the battle.[5]

The king himself entered the Tower of London with great fanfare and the whole building bedecked in his coat of arms and banners celebrating his victory. Although Agincourt had done much to enhance Henry's reputation, it was not a secure conquest of France, and the civil war between the Burgundians and Armagnac factions went on unabated, the latter being weakened by the duke of Orléans captivity in England. In November, Henry Percy was also finally released from captivity with the delayed prisoner exchange from July taking place and in March 1416 he was restored to the title of earl of Northumberland: the first person to hold the title for more than eight years. John needn't have worried too much about the restoration of Percy though, as although he held onto most of the lands his father had given him (some of which came from the Percy holdings). He was later also granted an annuity of 2,000 marks which provided him with an income which was more than adequate to retain his rank and dignity as duke and brother to the king. This helped him to retain his rank and dignity as duke of Bedford, living in the expected splendour. It would have more than offset any financial losses he might have incurred.

Battle of Harfleur

Agincourt was not the decisive battle some had hoped, despite the cost in terms of the sheer numbers who had been killed or captured, and within the year, the French were trying to take back some of what they had lost. In early 1416 an attempt was made to retake the coastal town of Harfleur spearheaded by Louis de Loigny, Count of St Pol, also known as Louis de Luxembourg, disguised his efforts behind a series of attacks on English ports. In one of those interesting historical twists of fate, Louis' daughter would go on to marry John, Duke of Bedford, and after his death, a knight called Anthony Woodville: her daughter was Elizabeth Woodville who became the wife and queen of Edward IV.

Henry and the English thought they had ended such things years earlier, but they were wrong, although Henry had had the foresight to leave a substantially sized garrison in Harfleur under Thomas Beaufort, earl of Dorset. Through the spring and into the summer of 1416 they were hard pressed by a blockade of Franco-Genoese ships, whilst Henry reassembled his fleet and got together crews to man his ships. However, by the time they were ready to sail he was unable to lead the fleet because he was by then engaging in negotiations with

Sigismund, king of Hungary, Germany and Bohemia for a mutual alliance against France. Thus, at the advice of the Council Bedford was chosen to lead the fleet.[6]

The events of that summer of 1416 deserve to be recounted in some detail because they mark one of two great military victories to John's name for which he is not often given enough credit. The fleet was initially divided in two, part was based in Southampton and part in Winchelsea, but eventually gathered together off Beachy Head and set sail on 14 August. The intent of this expedition was not to fight or engage the French, but to carry supplies in order to end the blockade of Harfleur, but in the end a battle did take place. On 14 August (it took only a few hours for the journey across the Channel) the two armies consisting of fleets filled with men spotted each other: on the French side there were also 'about thirty hired Castilian carracks' among the Genoese ships known as carracks. These ships known as carracks were reportedly huge, and dwarfed the English vessels; but what they had in size they lacked in manpower. More troops were aboard, but fewer were trained, and many hadn't been paid.[7]

On the morning of 15 August, a French and Genoese fleet emerged out of the misty sea in front of Harfleur. Bedford wisely sent out small boats as scouts before setting up a formation to prepare for the now inevitable battle, and as dawn broke, the thirty Castilian ships broke formation and sailed away. In the fifteenth century, naval battles did not involve an exchange of shipboard cannon fire as they did in later centuries. They mostly consisted of ships being boarded followed by hand-to-hand fighting more akin to that of land warfare. For many hours, the English and Franco-Genoese exchanged barrages of arrows, and slogged away in vicious hand to hand fighting. Perhaps 700 were killed among the English army but they eventually prevailed, perhaps by going around one end of the opposing line, or perhaps because the English longbowmen simply managed to outlast and outshoot the Genoese Crossbowmen.[8] Despite the English losses, including Bedford himself being injured, the English captured four

Genoese carracks after winning the battle and inflicted a considerable number of casualties on their enemies. Bedford sailed into Harfleur with provisions on his remaining ships having successfully broken the blockade to be greeted as a hero: what's more he now had four prizes to add to his brother's navy.

Yet, the battle might not have been the great victory the English sources claimed. The English had lost many soldiers, and twenty ships were sunk. Johnathan Sumption called it a pyrrhic victory, but one which achieved its aims of breaking the blockade of Harfleur and keeping the strategically important port in English hands as well as capturing enough treasure to keep the crews of the new ships paid for a year.[9] The French blamed their Spanish allies leaving for the defeat and it seems to have secured English naval dominance of the Channel. At home, and on the very same day as John defeated the French fleet at Harfleur, Henry signed a treaty with King Sigismund who became a close friend of his. Their agreement was intended as an alliance wherein Sigismund was expected to give Henry military aid if he needed it. However, Henry never called upon or received Sigismund's support as he was occupied for much of the rest of his reign with internal conflict in Bohemia and dealing with another 'heretical' group called the Hussites.

Henry received his brother the following day, On 16 August where he was staying near Rye in Kent. He was elated not only by the victory his younger brother had achieved, but also the validation of King Sigismund for his claim to France as well as a guarantee of military support for any future expedition. What he lacked was a decisive alliance with the duke of Burgundy which he wanted. Although Burgundy had not joined the French side at Agincourt, he vacillated in his support for England for entirely justifiable reasons. At least, reasons that seemed justifiable for the duke but not for the king of England. Before the end of 1416, Henry was planning another expedition to France. In December, Henry Percy was given the title that John had held for more than a decade, that of Warden of the East March. The 23-year-old was now responsible for the protection of England's northern border, and he was married to one of the daughters of Ralph Neville, to secure the power of the two families with an alliance.

The Second Invasion

Henry timed the sitting of the Lords in 1416 to coincide with the first anniversary of the Battle of Agincourt, and in the same session they granted him a generous tax to fund a second invasion of France. Although the Battle of Agincourt had been a great propaganda coup, it hadn't achieved very much in terms of territorial gains or securing the conquest of Normandy. The battle had been fought when the English were retreating and all the territory the English held onto from 1415 was basically Harfleur. This time, Henry decided to return with a number of important Norman cities in his sights, including Caen.

Once again, he left John in charge, leaving for France on 30 July 1417. He did not return to England for more than three years. Although this period is technically counted as the reign of Henry V, it is worth noting that John, Duke of Bedford effectively ruled England has his proxy for a total of almost four years. This entire period is worth studying, although it was connected with his brother's absence in France. John's second term of office as lieutenant of England was a lot more eventful than his first. First of all, he had to see off an invasion of the Scots. The duke of Albany and regent of Scotland gathered together a huge army with the intent of retaking Berwick and other unhappy border towns whilst the bulk of England's fighting forces were away in France. The previous year, he had travelled down to London because he heard that Henry V might be prepared to release his nephew upon payment of a hefty ransom, which of course did not happen. There is some suggestion that he was also swayed into action in 1417 by Lollard elements within England encouraging him to invade. Although this is unlikely since they were basically underground and didn't have ready access to the royal court.

In an event which became known as the Foul Raid, Albany and his kinsman the earl of Douglas built up their forces and then divided them in two: Douglas laid siege to Roxburgh in Northumberland and Albany's own forced attacked Berwick. Bedford soon learned of what had happened in London: and may have heard the insulting nickname which the earl of Douglas had begun to give him: 'John of the Wooden Sword'. This was of course a reference to the wooden practice swords which were used by boys when they were learning to fight. The insult was a jab at Bedford's prowess as a warrior which was ironic considering his record of over a decade fighting on the Scottish border. Bedford summoned troops to gather at Leicester, and the Northern lords also responded to his summons in short order, including the newly minted earl of Northumberland and his old friend, Ralph Neville, Earl of Westmorland. By 20 September 1417, Bedford arrived at Leicester and continued to move north; by the time he finally arrived on the border, however, there was nobody left to fight. Douglas and Albany had both withdrawn by the time he got there, cowed apparently by the rapid advance of the England army and by their own lack of progress. Sir Robert Umfraville had done a sterling job of defending Berwick, and Albany simply resorted to burning Norham on his journey back to the North. English chroniclers claimed that the Scots had fled before the advance of the duke of Bedford and his army, and he certainly achieved a bloodless victory which proved embarrassing for the opponents who had insulted him.

However, the 'foul raid' was fairly typical in the history of border incursions which very rarely resulted in major pitched battles. It is also unlikely that they fled in the face of Bedford but simply retreated because they had not achieved their aims of recapturing Berwick and other border settlements and didn't want to risk coming up against a major military force. It did demonstrate that Bedford was quite capable of co-ordinating a serious military response to threats such as border raids in his brother's absence one which, despite the absence of most of the country's armed forced had been enough to see off an ambitious incursion across the border. Bedford's army might have been more challenged by the type and size of armies who had been raised by rebels during his brother's reign.

When he returned to London, Bedford received more news: Sir John Oldcastle had been captured. The chronicler Thomas Walsingham tried to link him with the recent action in Scotland, but as previously mentioned that is likely to have been an exaggeration on his part linking heresy with the actions of the despised Scots and assuming the evil heretics were constantly sowing discord. What we do know is that the authorities wanted him to be punished for the offences that he had been convicted of three years earlier. John of Bedford would have remembered the Lollard rising and the alleged plot to kill or kidnap him and his brothers which Oldcastle had cooked up in the Christmas of 1414. Whilst his brother was besieging and hacking his way through Normandy, John finally came face to face with Sir John Oldcastle, the infamous heretic and rebel when he was brought before the Chief Justice in December 1417. He was brought before the Lords on 14 December which was presided over by John of Bedford and charged with treason, but this was not really a formal trial because that had already been held three years earlier. Oldcastle's response to being brought before the Lords was apparently to preach a sermon on the mercy of God; Walsingham, ever hostile to the Lollards claimed that he also said he didn't recognise the authority of the proceedings and said that if executed he would rise again on the third day. There is no other attestation for this rather shocking blasphemy and no reason to assume Oldcastle actually said it. Lollards may not have fitted into the religious orthodoxy of the time, but the vast majority of them were not the evil blasphemers that hostile chroniclers tried to make out.

Oldcastle's sentence was carried out the same day, as he was already a convicted heretic and outlaw. He was condemned to the unusual death of being burned whilst hanging at St Giles Fields on a specially erected hurdle. Bedford and other members of the Lords personally attended, along with a large crowd of people. John tried to offer him a last chance of confessing his sins to a priest and dying in the grace of the Catholic church, but Oldcastle refused and died bravely for his beliefs and his albeit erroneous conviction that Richard II was alive in Scotland.[10] The death of Oldcastle marked a rather solemn and sad ending to the year of 1417, but the people at the time would probably have interpreted it as a sign of divine favour for the punishment of a heretic.

Meanwhile, Henry was not only campaigning in Normandy, he also spent at least part of 1417 trying to find John a wife. One of his options was Jacqueline, daughter of the count of Holland who had been married to the dauphin Louis. Louis was the dauphin who features in Shakespeare's *Henry V*, although the bard failed to mention that he died in 1417 whilst still only in his late teens. Now she was a widow, and Henry sought a powerful alliance and foreign bride for his younger brother. Jacqueline wasn't just a great heiress; she was also the niece of the duke of Burgundy. Henry sent an embassy to negotiate for the marriage which fell through and she was married to John of Brabant, nephew to the duke of Burgundy whose father had been killed at Agincourt. The marriage was not happy, and Jacqueline never forgot the offer of an English alliance.

Henry's campaign which began in 1417 proved to be his longest: he stayed in France over three years, leaving John in charge all the while. In fact, it was one of the longest running continuous campaigns of the entire Hundred Year War. Reinforcements came from England under various lords to keep the things going with fresh troops from time to time, but the whole enterprise cost a fortune, and, in the end, Henry told his troops to basically support themselves. If this seems controversial, it pays to mention what Henry's plan was. He didn't just want to conquer Normandy but wanted to establish a permanent colony, rather like the Norman Conquest of England but in reverse. Many of the troops who came over from England were installed in garrisons in the various towns and cities which were captured. Many of these troops married local women, and established families in France, becoming not so much soldiers as settlers.

His brother kept him up to speed with events and some of their letters reveal aspects of their relationship. Whilst Henry undoubtedly trusted his brother and his abilities, Henry had an impatient streak. In November 1418 when he had been gone from England for nearly eighteen months Henry wrote a letter chiding his brother about seeing to the defence of ships in the Channel. This was essential for the provisions and reinforcements the king needed to maintain his campaigning, but some people had been violating the truces he'd made with the duke of Brittany (his stepmother's son), presumably by attacking French ships, and this meant there was once again a danger in the Channel. In a letter, Henry sarcastically remarked that his brother must've forgotten all the other letters he'd been sent reminding him of his duty. Henry enclosed a series of letters of complaints from Brittany with his missive and asked his brother to examine the letters and send anyone who had broken the truce to answer to him personally.[11] Henry wanted to focus as much attention as possible to his military campaigning and so could not afford to have complaints from his allies and attacks from his countrymen hampering those efforts. He didn't spend the whole of 1417–19 on campaign though, at least some of it was spent keeping up to speed with events at the Council of Constance which was aimed at repairing a rift in the Catholic church which had lasted for thirty years and had resulted in there being two popes, one in Avignon and one in Rome. Henry needed papal support for what he was doing in France and didn't want too many French bishops who might judge against him. So, he used his influence as a friend of Sigismund of Hungary to ensure the outcome which Henry wanted. Sigismund wanted him to work for the good of Christendom as he saw it and collude it the struggle against heresy. Henry was more interesting in working for English interests and ensure that the church did not condemn his actions or that a French pope and bishops would not take against him.

Back in England, John dealt with the day-to-day business of government; he must have noticed that matters in Scotland had settled down and heaved a sigh of relief. Yet there was a sting in the tail for in 1418 the dauphin of France began recruiting troops in Scotland. The war was going badly for France as Henry's conquest of Normandy was at its height. This dauphin was named Charles he was born in Paris, and was the fifth and youngest son of Charles VI and Isabeau of Bavaria: four of his brothers had perished before him, all had carried his title, and two others had confusingly shared his name. None knew it, but he was the one who would survive well into his adulthood, outliving all his brothers who died young. In the summer of that year, 1418, the English began to lay siege to Rouen the ancient capital of Normandy. Dauphin Charles had a company of Scottish bodyguards, and it was probably because of this that them he got the idea of recruiting soldiers from Scotland to resist the Norman invasion, though there had been an informal alliance between Scotland and France for more than a century. The dauphin's efforts paid off and between 6,000 to 7,000 men were contracted to serve in France, including John, Earl of Buchan, the son of the duke of Albany. Bedford would probably have learned about what was taking place soon afterwards, from spies or for his brother's contacts in France when the soldiers turned up there. The bolstering of French forces with Scottish troops might not have been a cause of immediate concern for either John or Henry but it would prove to be within two years.

1419 was to prove another rather eventful year for him. First, in February a woman called Joanna II of Naples decided to try to adopt John of Bedford as the heir to her lands. Joanna was queen of Naples, and titular queen of Jerusalem and Sicily. Joanna was a member of a cadet branch of the Capetians, the dynasty who had ruled France more than a century earlier and had once numbered kings of Jerusalem and Sicily among their ranks in the twelfth century and the thirteenth century during the time of the crusades. Of course, two of those three regions had been lost to long before and their titles were purely courtesy titles, except that of the ruler of Naples. By 1419, Joanna was in her late forties and childless. She had heard about Henry V the mighty victor of Agincourt and was seemingly interested in his brother John because he was by 1419 one of the richest men in England. He was now worth about 8,000 or 9,000 marks per year, four times more than the annuity he had been given three years earlier.[12]

If Joanna had made John her heir, he'd have become duke of Calabria with the expectation of inheriting all her lands in Southern Italy as well as any other territory he could conquer in addition to this. Henry V seems to have been seriously interested in her offer because he was always seeking powerful allies. Her offer came with a catch: John was to march to Naples within eight months and to bring 3,000 soldiers with him. This was because Joanna's family were regularly engaged in territorial wars and disputes involving their lands in Italy. 1419 was to exception as Joanna soon fell to fighting to reclaim her lands, and then fighting with the pope. Henry V and England did not have the manpower nor the money (Joanna also asked Henry V for a large sum of money as surety) to spare in order to interfere in the territorial wars of another kingdom with the vague promise of expanding their personal holdings. The war in France was enough of a commitment for Henry, John and the English parliament and people. John could certainly not afford to abandon his duties at Lieutenant of England in order to go off adventuring in some foreign land whilst his brother was also away. Although the negotiations with Joanna continued for another year, they soon petered out and she eventually dropped the idea of adopting John especially when the English ambassadors asked Joanna to grant John an allowance almost as large as the amount of money she'd requested from Henry.[13]

In August, the priest confessor of the queen dowager Joan of Navarre was arrested and had his goods seized. The following month, he accused Joan of using sorcery to encompass the king's death. This resulted in the confiscation of the queen dowager's huge dower of £4,000 which had been settled on her by Henry IV, as well as the seizure of many of her lands and possessions and the dismissal of all her 'foreign' servants and retainers.[14] In early October, she was arrested and imprisoned for three years in various castles.[15] The hysteria about witchcraft that is often wrongly associated with the medieval period was really a product of the fifteenth and sixteenth centuries and wasn't so prevalent in England as it was in some other European countries. Nonetheless, it had influenced perceptions in England

It was John, in his capacity as Lieutenant of England who had to oversee the arrest of his stepmother and presided over the investigation and punitive actions which were taken against her on behalf of his absent brother. Although she was never brought to trial, there had long been a belief that she was somehow compromised because of her first marriage to the duke of Brittany and her Breton children. Many believed that she was passing along information and even state secrets to her relatives and contacts in Brittany. These rumours had been circulating since 1415 or even earlier but had not been acted upon and the queen dowager had never been prevented from keeping in contact with her loved ones in France. It was not these actions which had been behind the allegations in 1419 either but the accusation of using sorcery to harm the king. The allegations were of course false, and may even have been trumped up by the king or by someone working for the duke of Bedford who had coached her confessor.[16] The motivation for the charges was almost certainly to stop payment of her dower, which was putting a strain on the exchequer and bolster the king's finances for his war in France. It was one of the most controversial actions of Henry's reign and one which he, himself, would come to regret, because he eventually ordered the restoration of his stepmother and her release from incarceration. This event though reveals the lengths to which Henry was occasionally prepared to go to restock his war chest.

Two more significant events happened in 1419 in France which directly impacted both Henry's war and which had repercussions for France and for Henry's brother long after they had taken place. First was the fall of Rouen in January after a gruelling and horrible siege which lasted for several months. Accounts say by the October of 1418 the population resorted to eating cats and dogs. Worse horrors were to follow as most of the civilian population were eventually expelled from the city: women, children the old and the sick. Normally the expectation was that people expelled from a city during a siege would be let through the lines of the besiegers to find safety elsewhere. During the Agincourt campaign civilians expelled from Harfleur had been allowed to leave, taking some possessions with them. Not so this time. Henry did not break the line to allow the people expelled from Rouen through and trapped between the besiegers and the besieged and many died of starvation. By the time Rouen fell, the only part of Eastern Normandy still in French hands was isolated outpost of Mont St Michael.

The conquest delivered a blow for the French, so much so that the royal party made moves towards reconciling with the Burgundians. John the Fearless, Duke of Burgundy was famous for his double dealing: whilst being officially allied with the English he had followed the dauphin's lead in courting Scotland to recruit troops. He had entered Paris in the summer of 1418 after having been previously banished from the capital in yet another phase of the decades-long civil war which had plagued France.

The drama of 1414 was replaying itself once again, and the people must've felt a distinct sense of déjà vu as his troops ran rampant in the capital, and murdered the count of Armagnac. Yet again, he failed to gain control of the heir to the throne, a different dauphin to the one in 1414 had escaped his clutches. Burgundy now has a choice to make: he could leave Paris to go after the dauphin, which would as good as hand the city over to Henry V, or aid Henry in his conquest of Normandy which would mean handing the city back to the dauphin and undoing everything he'd just achieved.[17] Instead, he went to the bargaining table and decided to try to make a truce with the 16-year-old heir to the throne: Burgundy and dauphin agreed to bury the hatchet in the interests of France and work together to drive Henry out of England. A furious Henry decided to respond in kind and sent men to take by ruse the town of Pontoise which was a mere 19 miles away from Paris. Fearing the English would try to take the capital next, Burgundy and the dauphin arranged another meeting to finalise the terms of their agreement. On 10 September 1419 they went to meet on neutral ground on a bridge 'over the river Yonne in at Montereau'.[18] Accounts of what happened next vary in small details, but not in the specifics. As Burgundy went to meet the dauphin in the middle of the bridge, he was apparently greeted by one of his attendants, a man by the name of Tanguy du Châtel a former provost of Paris who had previously been in the service of the murdered count of Armagnac. Burgundy then knelt to make obeisance to the dauphin and removed his hat, as per the custom. As he was still on his knees, Tanguy du Châtel cried out saying 'It is time' or perhaps 'Monsieur of Burgundy, take that!' whereupon he struck the duke between the shoulders with an axe, and then another man struck him with a sword in the face, more blows fell until he lay dying on the bridge, before finished him off with a final blow.[19] It all happened so fast that the duke's attendants barely had time to react, and they were either arrested or killed.

By the end of the day, the shocking news of the duke of Burgundy's murder had spread: the Burgundians said it was premeditated, but the dauphin said he was reacting to another attempt to kidnap him. With the hindsight of history, a Carthusian prior who showed the duke's skull to the king of France nearly a century after his assassination is supposed to have remarked that the hole in his skull was the 'hole through which the English entered France'. John the Fearless was followed as duke of Burgundy by his eldest son, the 22-year-old Philip of Charolais. He would be known as Philip the Good.

In England, John of Bedford presided over the Lords once again in October 1419. By this time the glorious memory of Agincourt was beginning to fade, and there instead a war-weariness in England. The absence of the king was mostly keenly felt in the Lords where many of the nobles' seats also stood empty on account of their occupiers being in France with the king. Five years of 'relentless taxation' had taken their toll, and the Lords were reluctant to grant the absent king another more taxes to continue the war even though Rouen the capital of Normandy had fallen in January of 1419.[20] There were also more reluctance by people in England to volunteer to fight. A possible explanation of this attitude is that the parliament of England and most of the people they represented weren't so much hostile to their king and to his ambitions in France, but instead that they didn't understand how his prolonged absence and the reconquest of Normandy served the best interests of England.[21]

After much wrangling by Bedford, they did grant a smaller amount of tax, but it was conditional on the king making peace with France within a year. That at least wasn't so hard to secure even before the death of John the Fearless, Henry V had been negotiating quietly with the queen of France to marry her daughter, Katherine. The king had been left because of his illness, but now Henry pushed forward not only with his plans for marriage but also to claim the throne of France in his own right.

He wanted nothing less than to be made the heir of Charles VI who would inherit the throne when he died. Henry was asking for nothing less than the total disinheritance of the dauphin and following the murder of Duke John that didn't seem so far-fetched after all. He was able to get the new duke of Burgundy and even Charles's own mother on side. Queen Isabeau's willingness to disinherit her own child in favour of the king of England might invite censure from some modern historians, but it shows she was nothing if not an astute political player. She backed the person who seemed strongest and who seemed to promise and end to the decades of internal strife which had plagued France for decades and already claimed the lives of so many of her relatives. Juliet Barker has remarked that in late 1419 and 1420 many in France shared her sentiments, seeing Henry as the safer bet and stronger pair of hands. This shows something about the dire political, social and economic state to which the country had sunk after more than a decade of civil strife: that many were willing to accept a foreign ruler.

Chapter Six

The English Kingdom of France

On Christmas Day 1419, Henry met with Philippe, the new young duke of Burgundy and with him made a treaty which involved recognising Henry as the heir to King Charles. Henry was receiving validation of his plans from all quarters before another, more formal treaty was made. On 21 May 1420, this finally happened. The terms of the treaty of Troyes formally made Henry V Charles heir and was supposed to create a sort of union of crowns. When it was ratified before the high altar of Troyes Cathedral, Henry also became formally engaged to the 19-year-old Katherine, Charles' daughter and his long sought after bride. Henry was 33, almost 34. His age at the time of his betrothal and marriage only a few weeks later was remarkably late for any medieval monarch.

Thomas, Duke of Clarence who had been with Henry in France for much of the three years since he left England formally swore to uphold the treaty and the following day a delegation of some 1,500 French dignitaries did the same. Eventually, all French people were expected to if now swear to uphold the treaty, then at least to respect and honour its terms. The young Dauphin Charles had been declared unfit to rule and a murderer because of his role in the murder of the duke of Burgundy. On the second of June, Katherine de Valois and Henry were married: the second Lancastrian king finally had his wife and consort.

It had only taken five years of war and thousands of deaths among her people and his own for the determined king of England to finally achieve and surpass his ambitions in France, and he must have considered his wife to have been hard-won indeed. Yet the conflict was not over for one person was not happy with the terms of the Treaty of Troyes and that was the dauphin Charles. In a situation which was to be mirrored in England some forty years later, the disinherited son of the king of France was being forced to fight for his throne in his own country against a man he saw (and probably rightly so) as a foreign usurper. Now his own family had turned against him, the dauphin had only his loyal followers to rely on, but he lived in a country that was still deeply divided along political and geographical lines and he was still able to command support from various parts of the country: the murder of the duke of Burgundy also firmly underscored his alliance with the Armagnacs. Those who had been enemies to the king of France were now cast as enemies of the king of England too and this included all aligned to and with Charles.

The Treaty of Troyes and the events of 1419 had not so much ended the war as committed Henry to the conquest of all the lands which belonged to the dauphin and to his political enemies as well. Henry did not relent in his efforts to oust the young dauphin who was now effectively striped of his title: within days of his marriage Henry was campaigning again: on 4 June when everyone else wanted to continue the marriage festivities Henry ordered them all to be ready to besiege the town of Sens. Back home, people must have been asking why Henry did not return now that he had completed the reconquest of Normandy and had his treaty as well as a wife. It probably hadn't dawned on most that the king was now committed to a subduing much more land and submitting it to his authority as the new heir to the throne.

A few weeks later, Henry sent orders for his brother John to come and join him in France, requiring him to finally end his three-year term as Guardian of England. He was replaced in that position with Humphrey, Duke of Gloucester. John had barely left England and now he headed across the Channel with 1,200 reinforcements in tow. He was also joined by Louis, Elector Palatinate who brought 700 German troops with him Louis or rather Ludvig a was not a random choice for he had once been married to Henry and John's younger sister, Blanche. Henry had asked for 5,000 men, and John had not even been able to bring him half of that number in a further demonstration of how difficult it was to recruit new troops in England. In England, the treaty of Troyes received a somewhat mixed reception: the Lords were still concerned that the implications of a cross-Channel realm, and the taxation which might be required to support it. They were also concerned that because of the union of crowns which it was supposed to create, with one king ruling over England and France it meant it meant the king would expend more time and effort in France than England. Three centuries earlier, when the kings of England had also been dukes of Normandy and counts of Anjou, a similar state had existed, but times had changed, and few wanted a return to a time when the king and head of the government had been absent for most of his reign.[1]

Why did Henry only send for his brother in five years after his first campaign in France and after having left him in charge in England for so long? Henry was not originally planning to claim the throne of France, but his goal of retaking Normandy had been met with the treaty of Troyes and his marriage: but the war was not over. Henry's decision to send for his capable younger brother join him in France may have been because he just wanted his assistance because he had upped the stakes. No longer was he just fighting for his ancestral possessions in Normandy but planning to become king of France and England.[2] Another possibility is that Henry had started to take the presence of Scottish troops in France more seriously. He asked that John bring 5,000 fresh troops from England with him, so this supports both possibilities. The dauphin getting reinforcements from Scotland resulted in Henry sending for Bedford and his choice to upscale the war effort.[3] It was the first time that John had left the land of his birth (not counting a few raids and diplomatic missions to Scotland): and he was to be involved in French affairs for the remainder of his life.

John also brought the long-since captive King James of Scotland with him, whom Henry hoped to use as leverage against the Scottish soldiers present in France. This plan hadn't worked very well before, and one wonders why Henry thought it would work again, but perhaps Henry was bargaining on the hatred that the young James harboured for the duke of Albany and his son sew division among the Scottish forces. The plan didn't work and instead the siege lasted several months. It seems to have been might have been at Melun or one of the other campaigns in France that the Scots started to use the unflattering epithet of 'soft sword' for John which was supposed to show that he was weak and ineffectual as a warrior: it was a nickname that harked back to his days as Warden of the March and the later abortive invasion of 1417 when John had not been able to see much in the way of pitched battles. Yet it is easy to underestimate Bedford's abilities as a commander: pitched battles were rare even in the fifteenth century. Henry had only been in two or three in his lifetime, and they were more than a decade apart. Bedford's strengths lay in planning and anticipating what his enemies might do next but the conflicts he was used to were on a smaller scale. Border raids, naval engagements. None quite compared to what he would encounter in the summer of 1420 at the siege of Melun.

Melun was a town less than 30 miles outside Paris. The prolonged siege included the unusual tactic of mining and countermining: extensive defences were built or shored up around the town and the English built a series of temporary structures around the defences. Beneath both were dug a network of tunnels intended to bring down the walls – the origin of the word 'undermining'. The English dug more mines in an attempt to intercept the French forces and at Melun there was vicious hand-to-hand fighting in these subterranean tunnels, including a duel between Henry himself and Arnaud Guillaume, sire de Barbazan who was the captain of the Melun. It also involved artillery bombardment, something which we associate more with the with seventeenth or eighteenth century, but canons started to be used as early as the fourteenth century in European warfare. The canons (known as bombards) of this time though were dangerous and imprecise items, although with an object as large as a medieval town wall it was hard for even canons to miss. During the siege, John spent perhaps the longest amount of time he had with his brothers Henry and Thomas then he had in several years. He also met Philip the Good, the new duke of Burgundy. Burgundy was 24, whereas John was several years older. The two men nonetheless seem to have struck up a friendship. Like John, Philip was a keen sportsman and a jouster, all activities popular with medieval nobles. He also shared John's love for books and the written word. Phillip, unlike his father didn't think he owed his main allegiance to the king of France and harboured ambitions to create an independent state from his lands in Flanders.[4]

When Melun was finally taken, Henry had a number of Scottish troops hanged as rebels against their king. Henry also wanted to have Barbazan executed as a traitor against his king, but the Frenchman managed to argue that he had only been doing his duty and that he should be judged according to the rules of chivalry and his death sentence was commuted to life imprisonment. Taking Melun had, more importantly, opened the path to Paris. Henry was received there with great ceremony and celebration where he met King Charles VI and summoned the Three Estates of France to confirm and ratify the Treaty of Troyes. The Three Estates were the French equivalent of the Lords, consisting of representatives of the clergy, nobility and commoners, only they were not a fixed institution did not always consist of the same people.

This meeting was summoned because people were already repudiating the treaty which had not provided the peaceful solution which Henry had hoped. His solution was to make all the members of the Three Estates swear to uphold the terms of the treaty again, and then have a prominent lawyer formally charge the king's son and former dauphin and his compatriots including with the murder of John the Fearless. The accused men were ordered to do penance for their crimes by walking barefoot through Paris and building a church at Montereau on the site of the late duke's murder. Needless to say, Charles and his friends did not appear, although one of those charged was the Sire de Barbazan who had been captured at Melun and who was by then a prisoner. He couldn't realistically be expected to adhere to the king of England's demands.

After Charles failed to materialise as a penitent in the streets of Paris as was expected, letters were issued formally declaring him and all who had conspired with him with treason, and formally barred from inheriting and lands or property. The declarations of treason also absolved any of their vassals of any oaths of allegiance or fealty to them and of any obligations, and lawyers suggested that a sentence of exile be passed upon them and all their lands be confiscated. If they were found entering Paris or any other place under the rule of the king of France they could be executed without legal penalty. Although not stated, it is a fair assumption that the penalty for treason would also apply to anyone who supported the former dauphin. The move was clearly intended to undermine the young Charles support network and potentially deprive him of his power base. He had become, by the murder of the duke of Burgundy and the treaty of Troyes, Henry V's most implacable enemy.

Henry spent the Christmas of 1420 with his wife and his two brothers Thomas and John in Paris. Later, commentators would accuse Henry of using royal revenues for himself leaving the incumbent King Charles to live in poverty, but this was not the case for money was still set aside for the king's maintenance. Despite the hardships and privations of war which had preceded them, the months that John spent with his brothers and new sister-in-law in France seem to have been some of the most contented of his life. He was not burdened with the rule of England, and his brother was finally planning to return home having achieved, it appeared, all he had set out to do in Normandy.

On 1 February 1421, Henry finally arrived back in his kingdom after an absence of some three-and and half years. He brought Bedford with him, leaving only Thomas of Clarence still in France. Bedford resumed his position as constable of England and was able to attend the coronation of Queen Katherine at Westminster Abbey on 24 February. Afterwards, Henry and his wife went on a tour of various shrines in the North of England. Henry and his wife's domestic bliss was not to last. only a few weeks after the king had returned an event took place in France which underscored the fact that the war was not over. We have already seen that Henry had left his second brother, Thomas, Duke of Clarence as heir presumptive and he was also left in charge of the English forces in France. This was to prove a rare and costly error of judgement on Henry's part. Clarence led a small English army of about 4,000–5,000 men in the tried and tested strategy of raids or chevauchée or armed raids through Anjou and Maine. These raids were intended to weaken the enemy by pillaging the land of food and resources and burning that land as a means of depriving the enemy of provisions and also undermining another lord's ability to protect his tenants. In late March, a small Franco-Scottish army arrived in the region near the small town of Vieil-Baugé to cut off the progress of the English, who were also camped nearby. By late March, their numbers had been buoyed by a force of Scottish troops under the command of the earl of Buchan. According to tradition, a Scottish man at arms was captured and he tipped off the duke of Clarence of an army about 6,000 strong which was waiting nearby. This happened on 21 or 22 March. The 22nd was Easter Saturday and the following day was Easter Sunday, the holiest day the Christian Calendar in which no self-respecting or pious Christian would fight. The story goes that against the advice of his generals, the experienced Sir Gilbert Umfraville and his cousin Thomas Holland, Earl of Huntingdon, Clarence decided on an immediate attack taking advantage of the element of surprise. He ordered another of his Lieutenants, Thomas Montagu to round up all the available archers who were scattered throughout the area foraging for food and accompany him on an attack.

Accompanied by Umfraville and a small force of about 1,500 men at arms, but with very few archers, Clarence met his enemies. The main battle happened on or just over a bridge, in which a small Scottish force was able to hold back Clarence for some time until

Buchan's men caught up. By the time the he broke through and got over the bridge, the full Franco-Scottish army of more than 4,000 men were ready and waiting. It is possible that Clarence and his men might have dismounted in order to get over the bridge, and then waded a short way through the river to fight on foot.

In the chaos of the resulting melee, and under a hail of Scottish arrows Clarence, Umfraville and the knight Sir John Grey were killed. According, again, to tradition the duke of Clarence was cut down by a Scotsman, Alexander Buchanan one of the three sons Sir Walter Buchanan. To this day, the badge of the Buchanan clan depicts a curious image of a hand holding aloft a hat: which is actually supposed to be a ducal coronet. This comes from an account which says that Alexander, after killing Clarence, took the Coronet from his head and put it on top of his lance, before carrying it in triumph. Several prominent men were also captured in the battle, including two of the sons of the Beaufort, Duke of Somerset. Edmund, then aged 18 and John, then aged 17. John would spend the next seventeen years as a captive in France, an experience which haunted him for the rest of his life and appears to have left him with deep-rooted psychological trauma. Although he later became duke of Somerset and was a notorious figure politics in the late 1430s and 1440s, he is most noted in history as the father of Lady Margaret Beaufort and the maternal grandfather of Henry Tudor. History has been unkind to Thomas, Duke of Clarence generally, but its most harsh judgement is reserved for his death and the fateful military engagement in which he perished.

Clarence is usually seen as impetuous and vainglorious, so desperate to achieve fame after decades living in his brother's shadow that he made a foolish decision to lead a doomed attack against a superior force. It may be that Clarence wanted to prove himself as a general in his own right, and the attack was certainly ill-judged and badly timed, numerical superiority did not always guarantee victory. Yet Clarence was not some young, unseasoned knight. He had been present with his brother for the three and a half years it had taken to conquer Normandy, and it seems unlikely that Henry would have untrusted him with command of all the English forces left in France had he not had faith in his brother's abilities. That faith, however, proved to be misplaced. Although Salisbury was able to lead a successful sortie a few hours later to rescue the remainder of the English forces, and to recover the body of the duke of Clarence the Battle of Baugé was the first defeat the English had suffered in France for a generation, and the death of the king of England's brother was to prove a major boost to the morale of the French. It proved that the English were not invincible, and it would in an indirect way change the course of history.

News of the defeat at Baugé spread quickly. Even the pope was impressed: it led to him dubbing the Scots as the 'antidote to the English'. Charles must have decided that recruiting Scottish troops a few years earlier had been the best decision he had ever made. He was advised, though not to rest on his laurels for too long and instead his advisors and friend urged him to press home his advantage and lead an attack on Paris with a view to reconquering Normandy. Unfortunately for him, Henry V had also received news of his brother's death and had wasted no time. He left his wife in the North and began preparations to return to France.

The Third Invasion

For the duke of Bedford, Clarence's death must have been an especially bitter blow. He had not only lost a beloved sibling, but the brother with whom he had spent Christmas only a few months earlier had died at the hands of a man who was the son of his oldest adversary. His brother had only just returned to England with his new wife, and almost as soon receiving news of Clarence's death he cut short his tour of the Northern shrines and made plans to return to France to resume the war against the dauphin. It wasn't just a matter of wanting to avenge the death of a brother, although that probably came into it but that what happened at Bauge underscored that the king of France's son was still a threat.

In June, Henry sailed for France once again and took the duke of Gloucester with him as he had on the Agincourt campaign several years earlier. Once again, he left the duke of Bedford in charge of England as he had before, but with one important change. Bedford was also officially the heir to the throne. He was now the oldest surviving brother of Henry and was the heir until such a time as Henry had a child. Katherine was already pregnant, and his brother might have known about it before he died but until she was delivered of a healthy son it was Bedford who would become king if anything was to happen to Henry. John resumed his duties as the proxy ruler of England in the absence of the king, and remained as such for nearly a year.

Once again Bedford presided over a meeting of the Lords, and this time the Commons were happier to grant taxes to fund the war. Why the sudden change? It is likely that the objection to a two years earlier had been due to the king's prolonged absence and not so much the war in France itself. Just before Henry's departure, a fugitive had arrived in England: Jacqueline of Holland, once the wife of the Dauphin Louis and then married against her wishes to John of Brabant. Jacqueline had made the bold move of leaving her husband, and had fled to England remembering how Henry had once sought her as a bride for his brother, and the former support she had received. She immediately tried to get her unhappy marriage to John of Brabant dissolved: of course, by fifteenth-century standards her actions were scandalous and shocking. Henry of England, however, not only harboured her, he even approved payments for her upkeep in England.

As already mentioned, Jacqueline was the niece of John, Duke of Burgundy, which made her the cousin of the incumbent duke. Phillippe considered his cousin's desertion of her husband a stain against the family honour. As such, it is remarkable that Henry supported her at the risk of offending his most important ally whose assistance was essential to his victory in France. Henry might have been intending to use her as a bargaining chip to give him and advantage in his negotiations with Burgundy, and perhaps gain control of her lands to 'strengthen the iron ring round France' which he was planning to create.[5]

On 6 December 1421, six months after Henry had left England for the third time the queen gave birth to a son at Windsor Castle. Finally, Henry V had his long-awaited heir, and it seemed a sign of good fortune that the child was born within eighteen months of his marriage. When his son was born, Henry was besieging the town of Meaux, and it was John who was the closet paternal relative present at the birth the child who was to become Henry VI of England. Bedford was no longer heir to the throne, but instead was godfather to the child, alongside his uncle, Thomas Beaufort, Bishop of Winchester. Jacqueline, who had become close friends with the queen, was the godmother. It is possible that one of John's illegitimate children by the unknown mistress mentioned earlier in the chapter might have met their newborn cousin at this time.

Henry received the news, probably from John himself, with the expected happiness. Yet in a savage twist of fate, it was likely that Henry contracted the illness during the siege of Meaux that was to kill him within the year. At the time of perhaps the most important event of his life, Henry's fate was sealed for the king was never to meet his son. The course of the war seemed to run as normal for several months after Meaux, and the king's son was christened at a ceremony which was typically lavish for the heir to the throne. Bedford might not have bene especially alarmed when, in May 1422, his brother was to send for him to join him in France once again. John answered his summons, once again bringing reinforcements and Queen Katherine to France with him. In her homeland, she was still only a princess, rather than a queen. By this time, Meaux had fallen into English lands, but it might have already become obvious in May that Henry was ill. He had probably contracted dysentery during the siege of Meaux. Dysentery was known as a soldier's disease because it was generally caused contamination of the water supply. Henry would not have drunk water directly, but he might have become infected in some other way.

It is often held that Henry summoned his brother and wife to France in May 1422 because he already knew he was dangerously ill and even anticipated his own death. I disagree. Even in the fifteenth century dysentery was a survivable illness. Humphrey, Duke of Gloucester contracted it during the Agincourt campaign and recovered, so why didn't his brother? It's possible, as Richard Wadge has suggested, that Henry simply refused to rest and receive the proper treatment because he was so focused on warfare. By the time he became too sick and weak to lead his armies into battle, it was too late. Ironically, Henry V may well have died because of his obsession with ending the war which the Treaty of Troyes effectively prolonged indefinitely.

On 12 June, at the request of the duke of Burgundy, Henry set out from Senlis where the court was staying to Cosne. He was used to travelling such long distances, but he soon became too ill to ride and made it less than halfway to his destination. He had to be carried in a litter to nearby Corbiel. It wasn't until then that the seriousness of his condition became apparent. He sent John ahead to Cosne whilst he lay feverish and gravely ill.[6] His physicians were afraid to give him any kind of medicine to be taken internally, lest it could not keep it down or it would make his situation worse. Considering the substances used for 'medicinal' purposes by some physicians, that was probably a wise choice. The extreme and dramatic symptoms of Henry's illness as well as its sudden onset have made some question whether it was just dysentery or of it was actually something more severe, perhaps smallpox or even the late stages of cancer. As soon as he received word of his brother's grave illness, John quickly left Cosne to be by his brother's side. Again, John had showed himself to be ever dutiful and placed his loyalty to his brother above the military objective. As far as we know, Henry wasn't angry with his brother, and there were other commanders at Cosne.

With little hope of treatment, Henry realised he was dying and with his usual stoicism, took to putting his affairs in order. He added a codicil to his will, made the year before which set out his wishes for the care and education of his son who was by then 8 months old. The duke of Gloucester was made the boy's guardian and Thomas Beaufort, Duke of Exeter was put in charge of his education. The government of England, though, was not placed in the hands of Gloucester – something which would later be a cause of rivalry and bitterness on the part of his brother. Instead, the dying king ordered that a regency council was to be created, consisting of several of the leading nobles of the realm who would rule until his son was old enough and would have to agree together to make decisions.

Henry did not, as is sometimes believed, nominate his brother John as the regent of France in his will. He actually stated that the duke of Burgundy was to be offered the position and only if he turned it down was it to go to John. The dying Henry also charged his continue the war effort 'until peace had been made or the whole country ... accepted the Treaty of Troyes'.[7] He also commanded his loyal brother to make no peace treaties with the dauphin which involved giving away any part of the Duchy of Normandy. He may have also asked John to maintain the alliance with Burgundy at all costs, but later changed his mind and just emphasised the importance of keeping Normandy for England if nothing else.

Bedford was one of the few nobles with his brother when he died in the early hours of the morning on 31 August 1422. He was two weeks shy of his thirty-sixth birthday and had died before his father-in-law the ailing Charles VI. This meant that Henry never achieved his ambition or intent set out in the treaty of Troyes to become king of France upon Charles' death. Nobody would have expected the man who had been healthy and vigorous only a few short months earlier to die so young, except perhaps on the battlefield. Henry, like his father had dreamed of leading another crusade to the Holy Land. At his death, he had a book near him about Godfrey de Bouillon which he had borrowed from his aunt Joan Beaufort.[8] Henry's death had denied the expected the heir to a European kingdom his throne for the second time in fifty years. Henry's body was sent in a procession back to England which lasted for over two months. Some wanted him to be buried in France, but in the end only his heart was interred there: Henry himself wanted his body to be buried in his homeland, and his coffin was carried to Westminster Abbey via Rouen and Canterbury.

On 21 October, Charles VI followed Henry to the grave. His bier was taken to the Hôtel Saint-Pol, a grand royal residence in Paris where the king and his family members lived for many years before being buried in Notre Dame Cathedral. In the space of two months the king of France and the king of England had both died. John, Duke of Bedford attended the funerals of both: at the funeral of Charles, he stood as a chief mourner dressed in black and standing in the place of the heir to the throne.[9] That heir was of course, either the infant son the English king or an embattled French prince depending on who you asked.

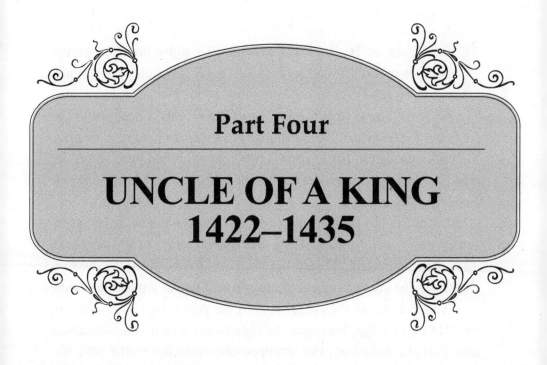

Part Four

UNCLE OF A KING
1422–1435

Chapter Seven

Regent of France

John, Duke of Bedford had lost his two older brothers within eighteen months of one another, leaving him the eldest surviving son of Henry IV and senior member of the House of Lancaster. We don't know what the impact of his brother's deaths was on John, but the demise of Henry might have been much more traumatic. Thomas had died in battle abroad, whereas John had been forced to watch helplessly as the older brother he idolised was brought low by a sudden illness.

Now, and not by his own choice John's future was destined to lay in France rather than England. He would seldom return to his homeland after 1422. Honouring his brother's wishes, John offered the duke of Burgundy the chance to become regent of France, a position which involved overseeing the kingdom until the young Henry VI came of age. He met Phillip 'immediately after Henry's death' at Vincennes near Paris to make the offer. Philippe discussed the matter with his counsellors and turned it down saying that he would leave the burden of taking up the regency to 'whoever was willing to bear it'.[1] It was indeed a heavy burden to bear, for the regent of France would be obligated to prevent a civil war and almost singlehandedly protect the English possessions.

Regent was a job that nobody wanted, yet John took it up with his usual determination and resolve. On 19 November 1422, John appeared before the parliament of Paris where he was formally inaugurated as regent, swearing to 'apply himself and all he had to the wellbeing of this realm and ensure that its subjects might live in peace and tranquillity'.[2] Like a king he then received the oaths of allegiance from all those present. John took his promise seriously, and instead of just being a war leader he tried to bolster the Norman economy by preventing debasement of the coinage. This involved adding non-precious metals such as copper or iron to silver and gold coins, reducing the gold content and the value of the currency in the process.

This was the least of the newly minted regent's problems though. The young Dauphin Charles had established his own polity which was centred around Bourges, where he lived with retainers and loyalists. This became known as the 'Kingdom of Bourges' because Charles was proclaimed King Charles VII by his loyalists following his father's death, and because he was ruling this territory in central France like a small kingdom in his own right. Since Henry V had also died, Charles believed that his most dangerous rival was also gone, and he could now seek to regain the throne of France in truth and not just in theory.[3]

Philippe of Burgundy hadn't attended the old king's funeral, instead choosing to return to his own lands in the Low Countries and thereafter took little interest in French affairs. In truth, Bedford needed him more than he needed Bedford because of the late Henry V's insistence on maintaining the Anglo-Burgundian alliance. In October 1422, only two months after his brother's death, Bedford began negotiations to marry Philip of Burgundy's sister, Anne, who was then aged about 18. The duke of Burgundy seems to have been very picky when it came to marriage partners for his sisters, rejecting various suitors or bringing an end to negotiations when he didn't approve of them. He was either persuaded or decided that duke John was a worthy husband for his sister because this time the negotiations didn't fall through.

Thus, John was betrothed to Anne in late 1422 upon which time the duke of Burgundy renewed his vows to uphold the treaty of Troyes, and they were married in either May or June. In an echo of his brother's nuptials barely three years earlier John, at age 34 took a bride who was only 18 or 19 years old. John and Anne's wedding was a grand affair, and also a dual marriage. It was intended to mark the creation of a tripartite alliance between John, the duke of Burgundy and the House of Brittany. Burgundy's older sister Margaret was married at the same time to Arthur de Richemont, the brother of the John III, Duke of Brittany. It is worth exploring Arthur's career to illustrate the important of this triple alliance which Bedford and Burgundy were trying to create and preserve. Arthur was, in fact, one of the sons of Joan of Navarre by her first husband which made him the stepbrother of Bedford by virtue of his father's marriage to Joan nearly twenty years earlier.

Although of course Joan had been forced to leave her children when she married Henry IV and there had been no real contact between her biological offspring and her stepchildren. However, because of the English connection and their mother's marriage to the king of England, both her sons held the honorary English title of earl of Richmond. Arthur had a major influence on his older brother and had firmly supported the Armagnacs against the duke of Burgundy in the civil war that had raged in France and had also been an erstwhile supporter of the Dauphin Louis (d.1417). He had fought on the French side at the Battle of Agincourt, resulting in his capture and being taken prisoner to England. His capture ironically resulted in Arthur being reunited with his mother after more than a decade. The boy of 10 that she had left behind was then a grown man of 22 and they were now caught on opposing sides in a bloody conflict. Joan, to her credit fought ardently to defend her son's interests and petition for his release when he was in England which might have been a factor in turning Henry V against her. Arthur was, eventually released in 1420 by which time it appeared he'd had a change of heart and a change of allegiance for he was instrumental in persuading his older brother to sign up the Treaty of Troyes, and two years later was, seemingly still on board. However, despite the ostentatious show of loyalty which this double marriage was supposed to represent, Bedford still didn't trust Richemont entirely knowing that he and his brother had vacillated before and wouldn't allow him to have any real power or high office in the new Anglo-Burgundian Regime. It proved to be a wise decision.

Bedford Hours

On the occasion of his marriage to Anne, Bedford gifted his new wife a beautiful, illuminated manuscript which is known today as the Bedford Hours. Books of hours were prayer books made for laypeople which allowed them to follow the monastic order of service. They were extremely popular in the fourteenth and fifteenth century as participation in religion by people who were not clerics became more individualised and varied. All of the books of hours which survive today all contain small personal touches reflecting the wishes or desires of the person who owned or commissioned them, and the Bedford Hours is no exception. It contains the coat of arms of John and Anne as well as portraits of both of them knelt before their favourite saints. It is rare to find surviving images of people from the fifteenth century who are not royals, so the images of John and his wife in the Bedford Hours is valuable and unique. It shows that John bore a striking resemblance to his brother, Henry V. He was tall and had the same dark hair as his father and brothers, and a large beaked nose. His hair was cut in the pudding bowl style which was more popular in England at the time and cropped at the back. It was a hairstyle associated with men of war, designed to not get in the way when they were wearing a helmet and is rather stark contrast with some of the longer styles fashionable at the time. John in the image is kneeling before St George, by then the patron saint of England and popular with the kings of England since Edward III.

Its not possible to see the colour of Anne's hair because of the elaborate headdress she is shown wearing in the image of her on the following page in the manuscript, but it might have been blonde. Judging from the image, Anne was of a petite frame and a pointed chin. She kneels before St Anne, who was most likely the saint whom she was named after, but there may have been more to the choice of St Anne than simply an allusion to her name. St Anne, according to tradition the mother of the Virgin Mary and is the patron saint of married couples and pregnant women. In the manuscript image she is depicted with an infant Mary on her lap, reminiscent of the images of the Virgin Mary herself holding the baby Jesus. Since the manuscript was a present from John, its likely both the images were commissioned by him. He may have asked Anne who her favourite saint was, but he also naturally hoped that he and Anne would soon have children together. Like his brother, John had married late in fifteenth-century terms and wanted to start a family as soon as was possible: unlike his brother it was not to be.

It may seem unlikely that John was able to have a full length illuminated manuscript of just over 200 pages in length produced in such a short time: only eight months or so elapsed between his betrothal and his marriage to the teenaged Anne. It's unlikely that the manuscript was produced from scratch for John. He probably already had the book and simply had a few more pages designed and created to celebrate his marriage. In fact, the order and selection of the prayers and passages in the Bedford hours suggests it was probably of French rather than English origin. Henry V acquired dozens, if not hundreds of books, when he claimed the French throne many of which had belonged to the French royal family. John seems to have followed his example and got hold of a few choice pieces for himself. It's even speculated that his Book of hours might have been made originally for the Dauphin Louis, who had been heir to the throne at the time of the Battle of Agincourt. Despite this, John should not be viewed as someone who looted French royal treasures. The re-use and modification of manuscripts was common everywhere in the medieval period, since books were so valuable. Bedford later came to be known as a patron of French monasteries, artists and poets.[4] He established more than one church in France and was later to commission French books and treatises. He probably also used French artists and illuminators for the work on the Bedford Hours.

Bedford chose to settle in Paris with his new wife, and although his marriage was no exception to the medieval aristocratic norm of an arranged match for political convenience, John appears to have soon developed a strong bond of affection for his young bride. Later on, Anne would become part of the glue which held together the Anglo-Burgundian alliance: a true peace-weaver in the early medieval sense of the word although there was no equivalent term in fifteenth-century France. As long as she lived, Philippe had no reason to abandon his alliance no matter how strained relations between her husband and her brother or their respective kingdoms became.[5]

Bedford was not left to live in marital bliss for long, as the continued hostilities in France soon took him back to the frontline. In the Spring, before his marriage he had prepared to besiege the fortress of Mont St Michel in Normandy, which had held out against the English for several years. He also had to contend with a Norman nobleman by the name of Jacques d'Harcourt count of Aumâle, who had not been reconciled to English rule and held the town of Le Crotoy against him as well as frequent raids and excursions by Charles and his men. He also had the eternal problem of getting money from the English the lord to pay for his troops in France. This problem was all the more acute now that he was the regent and was not directly dealing with the lord himself. If not paid, English soldiers might be tempted to forage in the French countryside but the problem with that was that if they took anything off local people in Normandy they would be seen as looting and since the Normans were now officially the subjects of the king of England their actions were deemed harmful and counterproductive. Bedford had a challenge on his hand to maintain the discipline among his troops to ensure he did not lose the support of the people of Normandy.

One of the ways he did this was by appealing to the Estates of Normandy for money and grants of taxation instead of to the

English parliament. Technically, the Treaty of Troyes had created an obligation for the king to raise his own money to support himself in France and to fund any military expeditions there. This money was to be extracted from his French subjects and estates. By summoning the Estates of Normandy John was allowing the local government of Normandy to pay for their own protection instead of relying on their conquerors from across the sea. This was also a good way reinforcing the notion of dual monarchy: at least as long as England was in a strong position.[6] Bedford, it seems planned to keep Normandy as a territory which, whilst ruled by the king of England, retained its own independence. It was not to become a vassal state of England but instead to retain its own legal, administrative and political independence. Phillip of Burgundy also started to contribute troops to the military campaigns in France which he and the regent were involved in. Bedford would pay them, or at least contribute to their wages, giving his army an important boost in terms of numbers if he was closely co-operating with Burgundy.

Gloucester's Marriage

Events in England were soon to throw a curveball into the regent's carefully managed plans and carefully maintained alliances in France. Sometime in 1423, possibly in the spring, Humphrey, Duke of Gloucester married Jacqueline of Holland, who had been a refugee in England since 1421 and had once been considered as a bride for John himself. The word of the marriage didn't get out until the October and when it did, it was greeted with international outrage because she was thought to have committed bigamy. Although she had fled from her second husband John of Brabant in 1421 and had been seeking an annulment of their marriage since before that time, she had not obtained a divorce; at least not one that was officially recognised by most of the church. The pope in Rome had refused to grant her a divorce from John of Brabant, so they apparently went to the schismatic pope

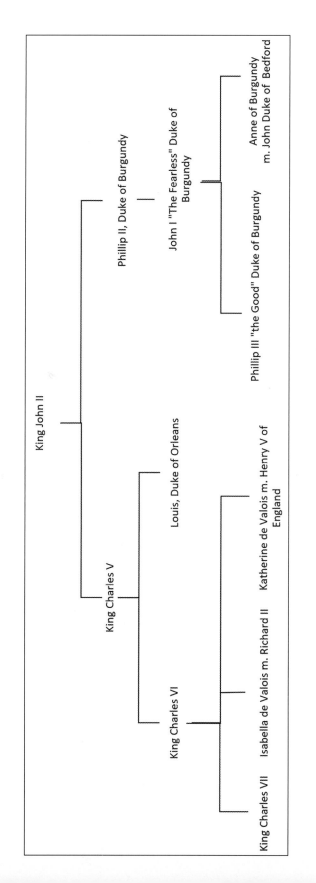

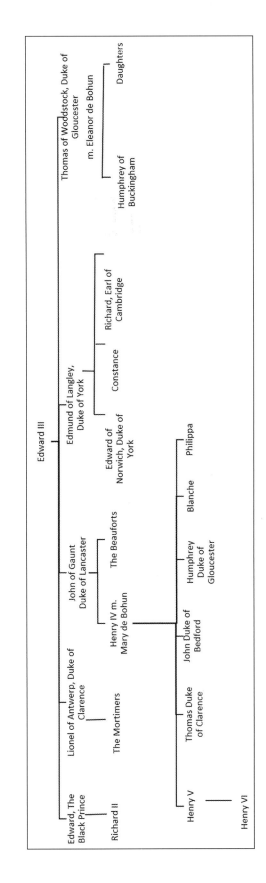

Right: The Gros Horlage or Great Clock of Rouen. The famous landmark dates from the late 14th century.

Below: Honfleur, Normandy: Looking out onto the harbour. Honfleur was captured by the English in 1419.

Left:
Honfleur,
Normandy,
view of the
River Seine

Below:
Modern image
of Joan of
Arc (centre)
and Yolande
of Aragorn
(right) in
Rouen.

Kenilworth
Castle, the
place of
John's Birth.

View from "John of Gaunt's chambers", Kenilworth Castle, Warwickshire. Most likely where John was born.

Above left, above right, and right: Illustrations from the Bedford Hours.

Above left: Side entrace of Rouen Cathedral, Normandy

Above right: Rouen Cathedral.

Left: Medieval Streets of Rouen.

Rouen, Medieval building.

Above and below: Courthouse, Rouen.

Joan of Arc Church, Rouen: sited in what is thought to have been the Medieval Marketplace.

Ruins of the Medieval Marketplace, Rouen, behind the Joan of Arc memorial. Reportedy the site where Joan was burned in 1431.

in Avignon instead. However, his rulings were not considered valid in France or in most parts of Europe, which meant their marriage itself was not considered legal. John of Brabant was the cousin of Phillip of Burgundy, and he naturally sided with his kinsman in the matter. Furthermore, Burgundy had territorial ambitions in the low countries and was intending to eventually subsume parts of Holland and Zeeland into his own lands. Humphrey, Duke of Gloucester was threatening to trifle with the wrong man.

John of Bedford could not afford to condone his brother's actions nor to side with him, regardless of what his personal feelings might have been. His alliance with Burgundy was too important. However, he also made to attempt to openly break with his brother either, and instead adopted a position of neutrality, even when Jacqueline announced her intention to regain her possessions, namely the counties of Holland and Zeeland, and the county of Hainault from her estranged husband, John of Bavaria. As long as it was just words and idle threats, John could still retain some degree of neutrality and adopt the responsibility of a mediator and arbitrator in the matter.[7]

This all changed in October 1424. On the sixteenth, Jacqueline and Humphrey landed at Calais with a small force, and the rest were soon to join them under the leadership of Humphrey's friend John Mowbray, the earl Marshall of England. Jacqueline intended to make good her claim and Humphrey was now calling himself count of Holland and Zeeland in right of his wife. This almost tipped matters over the edge. Burgundy had hitherto been resentful of English interference in his family affairs, but it was just that: interference. Little more than sabre-rattling and a slight against his cousin's honour. Humphrey's invasion threatened to turn a marital and familial dispute into a full-scale war. From Burgundy's perspective this upstart Englishman had absolutely no right to invade territory or lands which belonged to his family, especially in the name of a woman he wasn't legally married to.

Humphrey's actions in 1423–24 threatened to completely undermine the Anglo-Burgundian alliance. The power-brokers of the University of Paris wrote a letter to Humphrey in late 1424 which spelled this out, urging him to 'think about what scandal your perjury has brought down upon your head, what damage you have done to your king, what injury you are causing to us, what joy to your enemies and confusion among your friends'.[8] The perjury here was referring to their belief that Humphrey had gone back on his oath to uphold the terms of the Treaty of Troyes and the alliance with Burgundy which followed it. To the medieval mindset, perjury was not simply a dishonourable act, it was a sin against God. It was not Humphrey's controversial marriage that was the problem, as such it was the fact that he could not claim any legal, much less moral legitimacy for his actions. His army which landed in France that October had not been raised with the consent of the Lords, nor had his invasion been given the blessing of any authorities in France and England. He had acted purely of his own volition to launch what amounted to act of aggression against an official ally his family, his country and his king.

Burgundy was only within his rights to oppose Gloucester and his cousin's errant wife, he would have been seen as fully within his rights to distance himself from any previous alliances he had made with England, if not renege on them completely. Humphrey and Jacqueline's campaign in the low countries was initially successful. Within the space of two months, they managed to take much of Hainault and set themselves up in power at Le Mons. Their cause was aided by Jacqueline's mother, who encouraged some of their vassals in the Low Countries to accept her daughter's authority and renege their allegiance to John of Brabant and Philippe of Burgundy. Phillippe retaliated by launching a counter-invasion and raids into Jacqueline's territories. His troops burned villages, killing and robbing their inhabitants and driving many across the border as refugees. There was also a war of words between Humphrey and Philippe, with a series of strongly worded letters exchanged between them.

Jacqueline and Humphrey's forces eventually surrendered when besieged by a combined army of troops from Burgundy and Brabant, and the whole misadventure descended into farce when Philippe challenged Humphrey to single combat for impugning his honour. Humphrey accepted the challenge, and the combat was arranged for 26 April 1425: St George's day 23 April. The combat was to be held before John, Duke of Bedford. Philippe seems to have taken the offer of a duel very seriously, spending a small fortune on armour and training for himself, but in late March Humphrey retreated to Calais taking almost all of his army with him. From thence he limped back to England. Although he claimed to have returned to England to raise money for the duel, he never returned to Hainault, and had effectively abandoned the woman he married. Most of her army and her husband gone, and left alone with her enemies at the gates, Jacqueline surrendered by June and was forced to submit to her estranged husband John of Brabant to await the pope's judgement on the matter of her marriage. Humphrey's adventure had ended in failure and embarrassment, and, to add insult to injury, it was rumoured that he took up with another woman on his journey back to England. She was, according to tradition, a maid to Jacqueline by the name of Eleanor Cobham. When he got back to England, Humphrey did try to ask the Lords for more money to prevent his wife losing her lands to John of Brabant, but they refused, with his rival and Uncle Henry Beaufort, bishop of Winchester denouncing his actions in the strongest possible terms.

The debacle with the duke of Gloucester and the war the Low countries caused the duke of Burgundy to seriously consider coming to terms with Charles and even secretly negotiated with Charles envoys with a view to possible meeting. Gloucester's actions in 1424–25 almost overshadowed all that his brother had achieved in the three years since his brother's death. Almost. Although its ramifications were largely political and familial. It was harder to undo Bedford's greatest military achievement which helped secure England's holdings for the best part of a decade. To examine this in detail, it is necessary to look back two years before all that had happened in the Low Countries in 1425 and return to France.

Cravant and Laval

Charles the dauphin or Charles VII as he would have liked to be known, even though he had not been formally proclaimed or crowned king still had thousands of Scottish troops in his employment after the death of his father and Henry V. They had done him good service in the four years since he had sent his agents to Scotland to recruit them, not least at Baugé. Charles demonstrated his gratitude by promoting the earl of Buchan to the title of constable of France, and he hoped the Scots could demonstrate their effectiveness again. In 1423, he amassed a large army near Bourges with the intention of a large-scale invasion of Burgundian territory. From there a Scottish force of a few thousand others on an offensive into Burgundian territory: in the summer they laid siege to Cravant, which is now in Northern France but was then Burgundian territory. The dowager duchess of Burgundy, mother of Phillip and widow of John the Fearless sent word asking her son and his allies for aid. For Phillippe there must've been a feeling of déjà vu: the soldiers of the man who had murdered his father were attacking his territory and threatening his family.

Ever the good and faithful ally, John, Duke of Bedford hastily dispatched about 2,000 English soldiers from his base in Paris under the command of one of his captains, Thomas Montagu, Earl of Salisbury. He was the son of John Montagu who had once been a friend of John's father but had been killed in the Epiphany Rising in 1400. Many of the troops at Bedford's command were tied up in other sieges or the garrisons of Norman cities, and he could not go himself, so he had to send someone else. Salisbury had in fact been in France for only a few years longer than John, but this also meant he had more experience as well as a small army of his own.[9] Medieval lords typically brought large numbers of their own troops on campaigns: often raised from their own lands and contracted to serve them for a certain period of time although after several years most of the English soldiers in France were either being paid by the French government or they had effectively settled in France.

On 29 July, Montagu and the English army met up with the Burgundians at Auxerre and held a council of war. Two important things came from this meeting: first, Salisbury was able to ensure that the English and their Burgundian allies were absolutely in agreement and united when it came to each aspect of the strategy. He wanted there to be no disagreements or divisions between them would be disastrous for the planned military engagement. Second was a series of Ordinances of War which were drawn up. These tell us that the English and Burgundians were treating their army as a single, unified fighting force: the soldiers of the different nationalities were placed under strict instructions to live in harmony with one another and Marshals were appointed to ensure that the rules were kept. The troops were also prohibited from leaving their ranks without express permission from a commander or from taking prisoners until victory was certain.[10] Each man was also required to carry at least two days' worth of food with him and all the men were required to dismount and leave their horses behind the lines. At Cravant as at Agincourt eight years earlier, all were expected to fight on foot. Such strict discipline wasn't unknown. Henry V had issued ordinances but there isn't any evidence that the French or Scots had done do.[11] They serve as evidence that the English (and sometimes the Burgundian) army in fifteenth-century France were being treated as a professional fighting force. The strict discipline and tactical cooperation paid off.[12]

Despite a disadvantage in terms of numbers the Anglo-Burgundian army defeated a larger Scottish and French forces under the leadership of the earl of Buchan and John Stewart of Darnley on the last day of July. The Battle of Cravant was fought with the dauphinist forces consisting of French and many Scottish soldiers as well as a number Lombard and Aragonese mercenaries formed up between the town of Cravant and a river, and the English on the other side of the river. The English began by blasting their enemies with their canons, and then a volley of arrows from the 1,500 or so archers who decimated the front ranks of Buchan's army.[13] Following that, a division of troops under the command of Salisbury's lieutenant Robert Willoughby waded across the river to attack the dauphinists from the flank. With their Italian mercenaries beginning to panic and desert, discipline broke down among the enemy forces and they were finally routed when some of the townspeople of Cravant emerged from the town from behind them. The dauphanists lost perhaps 2,500 men, perhaps more. John Stewart and the earl of Buchan surrendered the Burgundians (probably not wanting to try their luck with the English). Buchan also had another problem: he hadn't actually been acting under the orders of Charles when he chose to lay siege to Cravant, and it might even have been a violation of a truce when had previously been made with the duke of Burgundy at a time when Charles envoys were trying to make him abandon the alliance with England.[14]

Cravant effectively ended Charles attempt to reconquer Burgundy for the time being, and more importantly proved the former dauphin's Scottish allies were, in fact, beatable. Since the death Clarence two years earlier, Buchan and his compatriots had been a constant thorn in the side of the English and a reminder of their costly humiliation. In their propaganda the dauphanists chose to play down their defeat at Cravant, claiming there had been almost no Frenchmen there and instead to talk about a victory at a skirmish a few months later near Laval in which John de la Pole was captured.

It was a great morale boost for the French with their commander the count of Aumale spreading the news all around and suggesting that a cavalry assault such as had been used at Laval was a certain way to defeat the English, who largely fought on foot. Short, sharp mounted assaults against undefended English position if they didn't have stakes driven into the ground to defend their positions or feared archers, it was said could be a means of overcoming the English foe.

John of Bedford sought to quickly repair the damage done by De La Pole's reckless actions. He had lost a brother in similar circumstances, and now history seemed to be repeating itself. Brigands, or armed raiders and mercenaries were clearly seen as a real problem and not just because of the havoc they tended to wreak in the countryside. There had always been bands of deserters or soldiers who chose to go rogue. John clearly realised the increase in brigandry after 1420 was due to new tactics being used by his enemies. John, after all he had years of experience from his youth living and fighting along the Scottish border. It would not have taken long for him to realise the French were probably adopting the methods of their Scottish compatriots and learning from them. Unfortunately, they used the tactic against the wrong man. John knew perfectly well how to deal with raiders. He appointed Lord Scales, another one of his commanders, to protect the towns and cities along the Siene and to prevent French raids. Bedford also managed to get a grant of money from the Estates General in France aimed at the 'extirpation of brigands'.[15]

John's long-term plan though was much more ambitious: he planned to expand England's conquest of France into Anjou and Maine. He came to believe that taking those counties would ensure the safety of Normandy in the long run. As a precursor, he sent English troops to take various towns and castles at strategic locations including Château d'Ivry-la-Bataille, or Ivry. The castle was besieged but eventually a chivalric principle called the *journée* was used whereby the garrison of a town or castle would agree to surrender it by a certain date unless their own side sent an army to relieve the siege by that date. In the case of Ivry, a date was set for 15 August 1424. At the time, the count of Aumale, the same man who had enjoyed success at Laval the day before was sweeping through parts of Normandy with much anticipated reinforcements from Scotland. Bedford was facing a war on effectively two fronts. Ivry then, became a sort of testing ground. The French were expected to come and relieve Ivry by 15 August and the English would be ready for them with their army there, hoping to engage them in a pitched battle. Such tactics had been used before: the most notable example would have been the Battle of Bannockburn nearly a hundred years earlier, in which the Scots basically manoeuvred the English into a battle when an English army came north to relieve the castle of Stirling which was being besieged. The English relying on their tried and tested strategy involving fighting on foot and using their fames archers hoped to be able to wipe out the Anglo-Scottish and secure the future of Normandy in one fell swoop by essentially trapping them and forcing them into a fight.

Aumale, though, wasn't quite so easily fooled. The French hadn't forgotten their humiliation at Agincourt and did not want to face the English army on their terms. He also hadn't forgotten what happened at Cravant the year before in which the largely Scottish and mercenary troops had basically been hemmed in between a besieged town and a river. With his Scottish reinforcements he did start to march towards Ivry, but did not have a number of Italian mercenaries with him. He also had the advantage of knowing exactly where the English were, whilst he and his soldier's location wasn't known to his enemy. The fifteenth of August came and went and the French relief army did not materialise. In truth, the French had allowed the castle to be handed over as a distraction, for in that very day Aumule's army had arrived outside the town of Verneuil some 30 miles south-West of Ivry. There, they engineered a clever ruse to capture the town without lifting a weapon.

The Scottish soldiers pretended to by English troops seeking refuge in the town. They said that the English had suffered a terrible defeat at Ivry at the hands of the Franco-Scottish army, the regent had been captured or even killed, and that they were survivors from the battle. To give their story more credibility, the Scottish soldiers even covered themselves in blood. It is interesting to note that the people of Verneuil could not really distinguish between English and Scottish when it came to accents, and that the Scots did not have to pretend very hard to pass as English. So much for the myth perpetuated by

Hollywood that English soldiers in the Hundred Years War sounded like Hugh Bonneville and the Scots spoke with thick Glaswegian accents. The gates were opened and Aumule's army poured in. From the safety of the town, Aumale sat tight and waited for his Lombard mercenaries to arrive, and the English close on their heels. The count must've been patting himself on the back for outsmarting the great duke of Bedford who he hoped to soon meet across the battlefield: at a place and time of his own choosing. Aumale had made one of the oldest blunders in military history, however. He fatally underestimated his enemy.

Chapter Eight

The Second Agincourt

When the duke of Bedford learned that Verneuil had been taken by a ruse, he moved quickly. Never a man to allow his emotions to rule him, any initial reaction of anger or shock was soon overtaken by action. Once again, he sent a captain to keep an eye on any other Anglo-Scottish forces who might be at large in the area, and then gathered together the rest of his army to face Aumale. His problem was that the Frenchman expected him, and so he had to plan his next move carefully. He soon learned, to his disappointment and anger, that the story the Scots had used to enter Verneuil had a major impact. Some Normans were actually abandoning their allegiance to the English, and throwing in their lots with Aumale. With some, it might have been an honest mistake purely because they believed the story of the English defeat, but others seem to have just used it as an opportunity to repudiate the English and side with their countrymen once again.

Having gathered up most of his army, John marched to Verneuil: this time there was no delegation. He himself led the army. He had come to meet not just Aumale, but the earls of Douglas and Buchan. They had been playing a game of cat and mouse with him for the better part of four years, and even before that on the Scottish borders Buchan's father had dealings with John. It wasn't a hate match, but there was a lot of bad blood between the main Scottish leaders and John, not least over what had happened with his brother, but also because of the 'Foul Raid' which Douglas had led into England in 1417. By 16 August, John and his army had come within 12 miles of Verneuil. The next day the English approached Verneuil through a forest, to find their Franco-Scottish foes already formed up: they had Italian or rather Lombard mercenaries buoying their ranks as before. The dauphanist army numbered, by some estimates as many as 14,000 men, with the English army numbering only 9,000 or so. However, it was common for numbers to be exaggerated or understated depending on who wrote a source, and what their partisan affiliations were. They certainly looked impressive: one chronicler reported that the dauphanists did not form up into separate groups with archers, cavalry and infantry in separate lines or ranks. Instead, they formed one solid and unbroken line spanning the countryside as far as they eye could see. This alone would have had the effect of making the dauphin's army appear larger and all the more formidable to the English.

Yet they weren't as unified as they appeared. The Scots argued about which commander should lead them with Douglas winning on the ground of his seniority. Insults and challenges were exchanged: in one prickly give-and-take, Bedford is said to have invited Douglas to have a drink with him, to which his adversary was supposed to have replied that he would be delighted to take up the offer, but it was a pity he'd had to come all the way to France to face Bedford since he couldn't find him in England. Douglas was as good as calling Bedford a coward, who fled from battle or resorted to underhanded tactics to avoid a confrontation, which was quite consistent with the previous insults the Scots had meted out to him about his leaden or wooden sword. Douglas seemed to forget that he was the one who had once fled from Bedford, when he had taken an English army to face his raiding army in Scotland, but such a show of bravado was necessary before a medieval battle.

For Bedford, it must have struck him as doubly ironic since not only was his adversary who had once fled from him presuming to rail him for cowardice, but the men who had deprived him of not just one, but two of his brothers now stood before him. Henry V might not have returned to France had it not been for Clarence's death, and might have avoided contracting the illness which killed him. Not only that, but in 1424 Bedford was the same age as his brother had been when he died: 35. He must have wondered at that moment if all his brothers were fated to be stuck down in their prime. Like most of his contemporaries, John was pious and followed the religious teachings of the Catholic church in which he had been raised. Perhaps he asked himself whether his brother's deaths were a sign of God's displeasure, but he would not have expressed the sentiment in public.

What was unusual about Verneuil is that both sides issued order for no prisoners to be taken during the course of the fighting, revealing the increasingly ruthless nature of combat in the Hundred Years War. Taking prisoners, whilst in keeping with chivalric customs and profitable could be a problem as well. Hundreds of enemy combatants, disarmed or sometimes not disarmed and with only a verbal promise to go on, were taken to a safe place behind the lines and expected to behave themselves until a battle was over. These could naturally prove an encumbrance taking up the time and energy of the troops. There were even cases of prisoners taking up arms and attacking those who had ostensibly captured them.

The battle finally opened, probably in the late morning or early afternoon of 17 August with a long tried and tested method: a salvo of arrows from both sides. The famed English and Welsh archers got within a bowshot of their foes and reigned down a hail of arrows upon the enemy infantry, killing but also causing confusion and dismay amongst their enemies' ranks. At Verneuil this was followed by a charge of the Lombard (Italian) cavalry. The battle was a close-run thing and very nearly resulted in a dauphinist victory. The 2,000 or so heavily armoured Lombard horsemen smashed into the English ranks from two separate directions: they managed to avoid the obstacles which Bedford had intentionally put in their path, and scatter the archers on one side. Then they managed to punch a hole in the ranks of the English infantry, sweeping behind the liens and causing chaos. At one point, a whole group of several hundred English troops broke and ran away from the battlefield, and with them took news of an English defeat to the surrounding villages. In the chaos, Bedford's standard fell down, which brought on panic and resulted in the belief that he himself had fallen or been killed. A standard, really a banner or battle-flag was usually held aloft before a warrior by his select man, his standard bearer. If the king or commander's standard fell down, it meant something bad had happened because someone had got close enough to him to seize or kill the man holding it. Such things had altered the course of battles before, and would do again – but at Verneuil a Norman soldier by the name of Jean de Sanne managed to get to Bedford's banner and raise it once again. This rallied the English men-at-arms who began to reform, and some archers were able to return and shoot at the Italian cavalry some of whom, considering their jobs done had taken to looting the English baggage train. Those who escaped this second barrage of English arrows fled back towards their own ranks.

A fateful decision was then made by one of the French commanders, the viscount of Narbonne to abandon his defensive position and order his men to charge at the English. The Scots followed, because they understood that a charge was most effective as a single amassed force of men and not in small groups or units. Their problem was that hundreds of fleeing horsemen were coming their way when they were charging, and the men crashed into one another. Although this was no deliberate killing in the chaos of the melee, the effect would still have been catastrophic on the French and Scottish infantry, with many troops colliding or being trampled by galloping horses. When the Franco-Scottish army finally did reach the English, they were in disarray: the single line of charging men had long since broken and the impetus of the charge was lost. Nevertheless, vicious hand to hand fighting ensued for more than an hour.

John, with his favoured weapon being the battle-axe was in the thick of it, as was expected of a commander and was surrounded by a company of his retainers and household knights. We don't entirely know what happened with his standard earlier on the battle, but he never seems to have been in any serious danger. His six-foot frame, clad in full plate armour with a coat of arms of the English royal family (which would have closely resembled that of his brothers) and wielding a battle axe or rather a poleaxe must have cut an impressive and terrifying figure in the melee. A contemporary chronicler wrote 'the duke of Bedford did wonderful feats of arms and killed many a man … he reached no one that he did not punish, since he was large in body and stout in limb, wise and brave in arms'[1] The part about 'punishing' here means that any enemy combatants who got near Bedford in the battle would have regretted it: but not for long, since he soon cut them down using his poleaxe. The weapons could anything up to 2 1/2 metres long, and had a spike on the tip as well as a hammer on the opposite end to the axe-head. In the hands of tall, strong and skilled warrior such as Bedford they would have been used to terrifying efficiency.

The vicious melee combat was what most medieval fighting men prepared for their entire lives, but most very rarely experienced: the chaos, and murderous bloodshed in the middle of a battle. Gradually, the English prevailed as the French began to fall back and as that happened, the English mercilessly cut and hacked down French, Scottish and Italian alike. As they fled back towards Verneuil, this time the town did not open its gates: the good people of the city could see very well for themselves the carnage being wrought before their gates and did not want to allow a victorious fighting force, driving by bloodlust and madly pursuing their vanquished enemies inside.

By the end, some 7,000 or more of the dauphanists lay dead on the battlefield, with the highest causalities among the Italian cavalry, who had initially achieved so much success. Most of the enemy commanders had also been killed: including The earl of Douglas, the earl of Buchan and one of Douglas' sons, as well as the viscount of Narbonne. John had that day, not only achieved and astounding victory but had avenged the death of his brother, Clarence and restored his family's reputation which had taken a battering in the last two years. He had also decimated the last great Scottish army in France and killed the men who had been responsible for bringing so many of their countrymen across the sea in the first place. Without

Douglas and Buchan's recruitment in their homeland there would have been few Scottish soldiers to begin with.

Verneuil is thus, rightly, considered a military victory as important as Agincourt, and is often described as the Second Agincourt. Even in the decades after the battle, it was described in similar terms and often mentioned alongside Henry V's great victory. In a day, John managed to destroy the Scottish forces who had been a thorn in his side for years, and to secure the English lands in Normandy for several years: yet his victory is not nearly so well-known nor so well publicised today as the battle his brother won on a rainy October day nine nears earlier. This is likely because John of Bedford was not a king and therefore his campaigns weren't considered as significant, but also because it was a battle which didn't have quite the same impact on morale in England.

Whereas the young King Henry had returned to England to praise and acclaim shortly after Agincourt, Bedford's victory and the campaign which resulted from it were seem as an exclusively French affair. The war in France seemed far more distant to people in England in 1424 than it had done in 1415 when they'd had to cough up to pay for it. Although reinforcements from England did occasionally go to France, Bedford tended to draw many of his forces from men who had been stationed in France for years, or had settled there. They were effectively men from the English colony in Normandy and their numbers were increased by Burgundian troops. Also, whereas Henry was bent on conquering Normandy, Bedford had up to that point been more focused on securing and protecting the existing English settlements. He hadn't gone to France as an adventurer, but as a guardian so whilst the people of England were pleased for him and for his victory it didn't impact them so much personally. They would celebrate of course, because Bedford had a good reputation and was still well-liked in England.

Although John was generally magnanimous in victory, and was becoming known at this time for taking a hard line against the excesses of his troops such well as looting of the countryside and abuse of non-combatants he did want to send out a message to his enemies. He had the body of the count of Narbonne cut into quarters and the parts hung on a gibbet in a gruesome reminder of not just his victory, but that he would not tolerate any opposition in Normandy. The county belonged to England, any who tried to rebel again would suffer a similar fate.

John did get a splendid victory parade: a few days after the battle he marched into Rouen, the capital of Normandy where he was greeted by riotous crowds. He was also greeted by his wife, who had been anxiously awaiting his return. Anne, it is said, usually accompanied John everywhere he went but she could not accompany him on a miliary expedition so this time he'd had to leave her in Rouen. The weeks before the battle would have been a tense time for her and any warrior's wife unsure if her husband would come back alive but after Verneuil there was cause for personal as well as public rejoicing. Rouen was festooned with bunting and the mighty victory was followed by a group of actors or models who recreated the events of the battle. He seems to have been consciously copying his brother, because he also had the Latin hymn *Tu Deum* sang in Paris when he paraded through the streets of that city in his triumphal return to the city he had made his home. His position was now basically unassailable: Charles could obviously still raise troops and command support but his designs on Lancastrian Normandy had been squashed and he had lost a good proportion of his army. His attempts to recruit Fresh troops in Scotland were hampered not only by the deaths of his allies Albany and Buchan but also by the new regime in Scotland. In early 1424, the king of Scotland, soon to be James I was finally released and free to return to his homeland. This happened as part of a negotiated settlement with England in the process, he married Joan Beaufort, the cousin of Henry VI and of John, Duke of Bedford. James was not in the least way friendly to his uncle, the duke of Albany. In fact, he took a hard line against Albany and all his relatives, seeking to crush their power in Scotland and promised the English he would take steps to prevent further recruitment of Scotsmen to fight for the French.

John, ever the practical man, very quickly consolidated his position after the battle to gain advantage of his victory. He allowed the French garrison to leave and replaced them with an Anglo-Norman one to ensure their future loyalty. At several other Norman towns, however he reduced the size of the garrisons, because the threat from Charles' Franco-Scots army had been eliminated it was no longer necessary to protect some of the border settlements, making it less likely that a ruse would happen again. Instead, he chose to redirect manpower and resources to other battlefronts. Several other Norman towns also surrendered because they realised Charles wasn't going to send an army to relieve them in the near future. Indeed, he couldn't put another substantial army in the field for several years after Verneuil. John was now able to focus his energies on the conquest of Maine and Anjou and presided over a meeting of the Estates General to announce his intention. As previously stated, John's goal in expanding his conquests was not only to protect Normandy, but also to take the war to the very borders of Dauphin Charles lands in the Loire. He'd been distracted from that before but was now determined to press ahead. He had planned everything down to the last detail and devoted the same number of troops to teach campaign: 1,600 to the invasion of Maine and Anjou, 1,600 to the garrisons in Normandy and field operations and 1,600 to the still continuing siege of Mont St Michel.[2]

John was thus able to ride high on the success of Verneuil for months and, indeed, years after the battle. It wasn't until October, two months after the battle that his younger brother, Humphrey, Duke of Gloucester, put a dampener on things a that John had to return to the world of politicking and holding his family alliances together. True to the mould of little brothers throughout time, Humphrey managed to be both annoying and inconvenient at once by interrupting his brother's intention to preside over further conquests in France.

Chapter Nine

Return Home

As we have already seen, between the end of 1424 and 1425 Humphrey, Duke of Gloucester managed to antagonise not only the duke of Burgundy and his wife's ex-husband (or actual husband depending on who one asked) but also managed to get himself into trouble in England. There was a little more to Humphrey, Duke Gloucester's actions than meets the eye, however. He had always been very popular with the people of London, who dubbed him 'good Duke Humphrey'. The merchants and power brokers of the city of London had a long-standing animosity for Flemish merchants and traders who made a home in the city. They had long felt the traders had too many privileges. This animosity led to them pressing Gloucester to take a hard stance against the duke of Burgundy, whose lands included parts of Flanders. The Londoners supported Henry's marriage to Jacqueline because it allowed Gloucester to challenge Burgundy and having and Englishman in control of the Flemish traders could benefit them. Gloucester's belligerence to Burgundy inevitably brought him into conflict with the duke of Bedford who was so dependant on Burgundy's goodwill and support. It also led to him butting heads with Beaufort, who supported the policy of the regency council which Henry V had created.[1]

Although Gloucester had been trusted with of managing affairs for a time when his brother Henry had been alive, the late king had not made him regent when he died. Instead, a council of lords and nobles reigned in the stead of the infant Henry VI of whom Gloucester was but one of many. Shortly after Henry V's death in 1422, Gloucester had tried to claim the position of England for himself using the fact that his late brother had named him as his young son's guardian to bolster his claim. The rest of the council which Henry had appointed of course refused him, with his uncle Henry Beaufort cutting the duke down to size.

When Gloucester returned home from his ill-fated mission to Flanders, he found that he had made an enemy of his uncle. Beaufort chided him for his actions and their quarrelling caused a rift in the council which was supposed to rule the country on behalf of the 4-year-old King Henry VI. The dispute grew into a cold war between then for control of the council and person of the young king, and by October 1425 Beaufort decided to write to John, Duke of Bedford to beg for him to return home to England to put an end to the dispute.

Bedford had by that point been absent from England for three-and-a-half years, that is since his late brother Henry had sent for him in July 1422. Yet despite his long absence, John was still considered the most senior and most trusted members of the royal family. Even though his Uncle Beaufort was many years older than him, John had more direct and recent experience of running the government than either the bishop of Winchester or his brother Gloucester. Beaufort feared that the political turmoil in England could negatively affect the dual monarchy, as the English claim to the throne of France had become known.

So, in the closing week of 1425 or early 1426, the regent of France set sail for his homeland once again accompanied by his wife Anne. Upon his arrival, Bedford initially stayed at Westminster Palace where he and Anne met with his nephew, the young King Henry VI. When John had last seen the child, Henry had only been a few months old. By this time, he was 4 and able to converse with his famous uncle. It must have been somewhat awkward for a tall man in his late thirties to kneel to a mere child, the age of a modern preschooler sitting on a throne far too large for him. Nevertheless, such were the ceremonies and customs of medieval kingship.

It was the first time the duke of Burgundy's sister had ever seen England, and met the young king. At 21, the duchess of Bedford was still a very young woman, and she proved a popular and well-loved figure at court. She was the closest thing to queen: Humphrey, Duke of Gloucester had left his wife in the Low Countries and had shacked up with Eleanor Cobham, but could not marry her. Anne may have had a chance to meet the young king's mother Katherine who was also her cousin. Katherine was only a few years older than her at 24. Katherine had taken up residence at Wallingford Castle in Berkshire (today Oxfordshire) rather than in London, but the two women had much in common with their marriages into the English royal family to forge alliances which both had their origins at a time of brutal civil strife in France. After nearly three years of marriage to John, there was no sign of any children for Anne yet, but she was still young even by medieval standards and so it might not have been too much of a concern at that point. John did, however, have an illegitimate daughter named Marie or Maria (the name is rendered in several different ways) by an unknown mistress. She was born a few years before his marriage to Anne.

Although the exact date of her birth is unknown, it appears to have been about 1420 or sometime shortly after: late in the reign of Henry V and perhaps between the two occasions in which Bedford had first been summoned to France. Like her father, her future lay across the Channel. The relationships between medieval queens and noblewomen and the children their husbands sired upon other women before or during their marriages could be fraught and difficult, but they could also go the other way. The total lack of evidence for her mother, as well as the fact that she seemed to have grown up in her father's household from a young age suggests that Marie's mother might have died when she was only was a baby or an infant. Anne might have become something like a stepmother figure to the young girl.

Meanwhile, John performed the ceremonial duty of knighting the young Henry VI. This was a duty which was normally performed by adult kings who knighted their sons and heirs but everything about

Henry's case was unusual. In February 1426, he attended the opening of the Lords in Leicester Castle. His goal was to persuade the Lords to accept that the war in France was still England's business and not just a 'foreign adventure by the House of Lancaster'.[2] Before that though, he had to deal with his brother's dispute in the Lords. Members of the Lords had to be reminded to leave their weapons at home, and the whole proceeding was relocated to Leicester because of the dangerous atmosphere in London. Gloucester sulked in his chambers when it opened, before eventually emerging to present a series of charges against his uncle. His uncle in turn asked commissioners to adjudge his marriage to Jacqueline to be adulterous. Beaufort was eventually exonerated of all charges in a proclamation made before the young king, but he was made to resign his office as chancellor. The two were forced to make a public gesture of friendship and reconciliation by clasping hands.

Afterwards, John was to learn that his brother's expedition to the Low Countries the previous year had used up so much money and energy that there was barely enough left to fund the continuing war in France. Gloucester had borrowed huge amounts of money from various members, the very people who would have provided tax money. Although he was able to obtain some money and soldiers from the Estates and government in Normandy, and could rely on the duke of Burgundy for support at times, neither source was entirely reliable. He needed the Lords to support his efforts, but they ruled out even trying to raise any more troops for months. The forces which had been sent to France had been financed by loans and borrowed money and that could not go on forever. Or else the Commons simply did not want to lend anymore of their money. Loans had to be repaid. In the end, John and the Lords ordered a review of the government's finances. This unusual move involved exchequer records being brought up from Westminster to Leicester for inspection: this most have been a monumental task, since these records consisted of huge rolls of parchment.

The review just proved what was already known: there wasn't enough money to raise a large army for John and since the chancellor had resigned, there was no way to get it except if the Lords voted for one, which they were not willing to do. In the end, John was forced to resort to penny-pinching and redirecting money away from other things, including the Calais garrison. Although he did try to solve the problem in long run by having his own men installed as the chancellor and the treasurer. Both of these positions though were temporary appointments and could only help him so much.

John wanted to return to France as early as June 1426, but as long as the Lords refused to raise the money for a new expeditionary army to aid his conquest of Maine and Anjou, he was not prepared to do so. So, he stayed. In early June, he and Anne visited the shrine of St Alban, and then made a circuit of various religious sites and shrines in the Midlands and North of England. In the end, business in England kept John and Anne in the country for more that fifteen months. This included keeping a reign on his brother's activities and preventing him from sending any more money or troops to Jacqueline who was still fighting against the duke of Burgundy. Even though he had effectively abandoned her in another country, Gloucester still claimed he wanted to help the woman he married and does seem to have tried to raise money several times, before being prevented from first his uncle and then his brother. Yet their marriage was, to all intents and purposes, over as soon as he had returned home to England in 1425. Nevertheless, Humphrey felt increasingly resentful of his brother. Although he didn't actively try to oppose him, he did write about how he would go back to ruling and doing has he wished as soon as his John returned to France. John must've been saddened by the breakdown of his relationship with his only surviving brother but knew that thwarting any ambitions Humphrey held were essential to the security of Normandy. A cause to which he was entirely devoted.

When he and Anne finally returned to France, it was not until late March 1427. He was determined to bring the duke of Brittany, who had abandoned his allegiance to England, to heel. Bedford was able to get the duke and his sons to submit to him again in 1427, but the duke always vacillated and ruled over a duchy and family which were deeply divided: shortly after hearing about the submission the dauphin tried to encourage him to change sides once again. He wouldn't do that as long as Bedford was in the strongest position.

That very same month, John received a letter from the council in England, urging him to accept that his brother's previous attempts to send aid to Jacqueline had been valid. He'd spent more than a year in England trying to prevent such things and claw back as much money as possible: and then the moment his back was turned they began to completely ignore his wishes again. The council said that the people of England had long since taken Jacqueline's cause to heart: this was used to justify one more loan to Gloucester on the proviso that he used it for nothing other than to raise troops to send to her aid. The very same council which had refused to provide money for him to take troops to France had once again proved willing to do this for his brother's personal venture. Popularity had once again trumped what Bedford saw as political necessity. Gloucester was even able to win some other nobles to his side including the veteran earl of Salisbury. Bedford probably feared he'd have to return home again, but in the event, he sent to emissaries to England with a personal letter for his brother. The letter was a desperate attempt to appeal to Gloucester's loyalty to the young king, their nephew and urged him to pursue his ends by means of a peaceful settlement instead of by violence. This time, Gloucester heeded his brother's advice.

Six months later, the pope finally issued his judgement in the matter concluding that Jacqueline's marriage to John of Brabant (who died in April 1427) was valid and that her marriage to the duke of Gloucester had been bigamous all along, and never legal. There was no arguing with the pope's decision and no point in prolonging the matter. Finally, after five years of war, division and disputation Gloucester accepted that his marriage had never been valid and lost all interest in Jacqueline. Weeks afterwards, he married his mistress of several years, Eleanor Cobham. The debacle over his marriage though, did have one unfortunate personal consequence for Humphrey. He and Eleanor had two children together, but because both were born before their marriage they were counted as illegitimate and she was, apparently, unable to have any further children afterwards.

There was, similarly, no sign of any children with Anne for John. He might not have been too worried since John's focus had always been on his activities in France: his personal life and perpetuating his own legacy always took something of a back foot. After forcing the duke of Brittany to submit to him and when the matter of his brother's marriage was finally dealt with, John once again returned his attention to his campaign in Maine and Anjou. That which kept being delayed or had to be led by others because his presence had been required elsewhere. He had now brought from England new soldiers and a new commander: John, Lord Talbot.

Talbot had years of experience fighting in Wales and Ireland, where he had gained a reputation for brutality and harshness. John of course, did not share such a reputation and was known for being fairer, at least in Normandy and unless he was crossed or felt betrayed. New commanders also meant different approaches and strategies. Although all the new commanders were technically subject to the regent, they had a lot of autonomy. Although John adopted a policy in Normandy of treating the people as the subjects of the English king who should be respected and not abused or mistreated, his commanders did not extend this policy to other parts of France. In Maine and Anjou, the people were to be treated as enemy combatants and conciliation was most assuredly not the order of the day. A notorious new commander like Talbot in tow and a newer, tougher policy being adopted to expand the conquest of France spelled doom for the English in the end. Little did John or anyone else know, but when the new year of 1428 dawned, the tide of the war would finally turn against them.

The Siege of Orléans

Historians seeking the real turning point for English fortunes in later part of the Hundred Years War might well point to the siege of the city of Orléans. Orléans is situated far outside the bounds of Normandy and the decision to try and take it was part of an aggressive strategy aimed at taking on the dauphin Charles in his own territory. No more would the English wait for raids and incursions into Normandy or try to protect and defend the borders of that Duchy.

The decision to move on Orléans was the brainchild of the earl of Salisbury, a friend of John who had previously been his erstwhile ally. Before John had departed for England in 1426, Salisbury had almost never questioned him nor pushed his own policies and ideas, but now he did. It is possible that the duke of Gloucester had influenced him in this regard to get back at his brother for opposing his marriage and his plans in the Low Countries. What we do know is that John never supported the attempt to capture the city in the Loire Valley, even though he was eventually forced to provide financial and military backing for the siege. In fact, Salisbury did not let Bedford know of his plans in advance and basically sprung them on him unexpectedly when he arrived back in France in 1428. John was uncomfortable with the plan for strategic reasons, because of the overreach involved. The English were already involved in military campaigns in Maine and Anjou, and it would be stretching their manpower and resources too far and too thinly. The duke of Burgundy also harboured ambitions in the Loire Valley, and he chose to interpret the English campaign there yet another attempt to thwart him. After having had to shore up the Anglo-Burgundian alliance following the slap in the face his brother had delivered to the duke of Burgundy, the English risked offending him yet again. Finally, the siege was an offense against the code of chivalry because the duke of Orléans who was supposed to have been responsible for the defence and maintenance of the city had been a prisoner in England for thirteen years. He was captured at Agincourt, and nobody was talking about releasing him.

Grudgingly, Bedford marched to Orléans in the late summer of 1428 to undertake a brutal and gruelling siege which would last for many months, already questioning the wisdom of the enterprise before he had even started. Far away to the Northeast lay a small, insignificant village called Domrémy. Neither Salisbury, nor Bedford nor anyone else had even heard of the place, and it certainly would not have warranted their attention. There, among the fields and farms lived a teenage peasant girl with her family. This peasant girl, however, was set apart from her peers. Although she was only 16 or 17 years of age, she claimed to have visions from God. She said that she saw saints and was visited by angels when in church or even doing her work and labours around the farm. Her name was Joan.

Chapter Ten

The Regent and the Maid

T he girl who was known to history as Joan of Arc first emerged into history when she was introduced to the court of the Dauphin Louis, or Charles VII in early 1429, but her story really began earlier than that. Normally, a peasant girl who claimed to have had visions about a member of the royal family would not have elicited that much attention. They might have just been brought to court once, heard, and then dismissed accordingly. Joan's visions, however, came at a time when they were most needed in France and could be used to the political advantage of those in power. This may seem like an overly cynical view of events, but from the very beginning Joan of Arc had powerful political backers without whom she could never have achieved the fame and position that she did.

Joan first arrived at the siege of Orléans, which was to become one of the most infamous events of the Hundred Years War. It lasted for many months. The length of the siege, which tested English resources to its limit, dragged out over the winter of 1428–29. The situation was not helped when on 24 October 1428 the earl of Salisbury who had been presiding over the siege was involved in a freak accident. He was standing in a fortress, overlooking one of the bridgeheads which led into the city when a cannonball struck a wall near to him, and the earl was trapped in the falling masonry. Although he survived, half of his face caved in, and Salisbury died eight days later. England had lost one of her best commanders: he was replaced with the earl of Suffolk who, whilst capable, 'had little of Salisbury's daring or charisma'.[1] Much of the impetus for taking the city was lost, as well as the cause for doing so because the whole project had been Salisbury's brainchild.

The siege also underscored the political divisions which were becoming more obvious in France. The duke of Burgundy felt personally offended by the English-run siege, not because of any affection for the duke of Orléans, but because he felt that this, too, threatened his interests. Burgundy wanted to be appointed as the official guardian of the city, because the duke was a prisoner in England, but if that was to be done, it meant the English would have to give up on the idea of taking the city altogether or accept its surrender to Burgundy.

As was normal when he felt threatened, Burgundy began to make approaches to Charles of France or vice versa. The difference in 1428–29 though was that he began to openly engage in negotiations with the self-styled king of France, and with the king's formidable mother-in-law, Yolande of Aragon. Charles married her daughter, Marie of Anjou in 1422 and Yolande became one of Charles closest allies and advisors, often taking charge of political and diplomatic affairs and fully invested in serving the interests of the exiled French prince and the war against the English.[2]

It was Yolande who had brokered the deal between the duke of Brittany and his brother, Arthur de Richemont and Charles in 1425, and she seems to have been the person who 'discovered' Joan of Arc. Or rather one of her servants. She knew about her weeks before Joan was presented to the royal court at Chinon in February 1429, and possibly had heard about her the previous year when she had approached the captain of Vaucouleurs, a small walled town only ten miles away from her hometown of Domrémy, asking to be taken to the king with a message from God. At first, the captain sent her away with a flea in her ear, but a few months later, when she came back, the young girl's words began to attract the attention of the powerful.

So, Yolande heard of her and ensured she was brought to court where Joan was forced to undergo a series of rigorous 'tests' – first of her religious orthodoxy and then to ensure that she was a virgin as she claimed. The second would have been especially humiliating and personal, but Joan was prepared to undertake them all and apparently passed them all. From her earliest days though, Joan wore men's clothes and had her hair cut short: it was a bold and controversial action, but bolder were her words. Joan proclaimed that she had been sent by God himself to wage war on the English and free France. They were the words that Charles and his court needed to hear after years of being on the back foot and still feeling the sting of repeated defeats, the idea that God was turning his favour to France once again was not just inspirational, it was revolutionary.

Having gone through the tests, interrogations and questions of the learned clerics at court, Joan lost none of her spirit. She repeatedly stated that her mission was to have the true king, Charles, crowned at Riems and when she was reminded that Orléans lay in her way, Joan asserted that they could determine whether she had really been sent by God by sending her personally to lift the siege. Joan had no doubt in her own ability: it could have been the simple hubris and reckless confidence of her youth, or maybe Joan really had heard from God. From a modern perspective looking at the historical context, it's likely that she had been coached or encouraged for some time. No doubt Joan believed sincerely in her visions, but it's not impossible she was influenced by those around her.

Surprisingly, Charles allowed Joan to have her way. After sending a letter addressed to the English commanders including the duke of Bedford telling them to go home or face the wrath of the almighty:

> King of England, and you, Duke of Bedford, who call yourself Regent of the kingdom of France; you, William de la Pole, Earl of Suffolk; John Lord Talbot; and you, Thomas Lord Scales, who call yourselves lieutenants of the said Duke of Bedford, make satisfaction to the king of Heaven; surrender to the Pucelle, who has been sent here by God, the king of Heaven, the keys of all the good towns that you have taken and violated in France . . . And

you too, archers, companions-at-arms, gentlemen and others who are before the town of Orléans, go back to your own country, by God. And if you do not do this, await news of the Pucelle who will come to see you shortly, to your very great harm. King of England, if you do not do this, I am commander of war, and in whatever place I come upon your men in France, I will make them leave, whether they wish to or not. And if they do not wish to obey, I will have them all killed; I have been sent here by God, the king of Heaven, to drive you out of all France, body for body. And if they wish to obey, I will show them mercy.[3]

Following the letter, which she dictated to a scribe because Joan herself was illiterate, Joan was sent to Orléans with a small escort. On 29 April she entered at the head of a baggage train bringing supplies. However, the traditional view of how things went at Orléans isn't strictly true. The evidence reveals that shortly before Joan was unleashed on the city, the duke of Burgundy had tried to negotiate for Orléans to be handed over to him, with half the revenue to be given to the king of England. Bedford refused it, but the siege had already suffered grave setbacks with the death of Salisbury and the garrison's contracts to serve having expired. Joan's entry into Orléans was carefully planned and prepared by others. All of this gives the impression that Joan of Arc's entry into the fray at Orléans was carefully stage-managed by the political elite. It wasn't so much a miracle, at the planned deployment of a new secret weapon in France's arsenal. That deployment proved to be highly successful because within four days of Joan's entry the siege of Orléans was ended, but even then, it was not the dramatic event which some contemporary chroniclers wanted people to think.

The English war effort had already been compromised by the death of Salisbury, and the ones who remained at the siege were exhausted or their contracts to serve had expired. Some French sources said the arrival of Joan of Arc caused mass desertions among the English, but the desertions seem to have come before that, and resulted from Salisbury's demise. Salisbury's men probably didn't consider themselves obliged to serve the earl of Suffolk or continue to serve in a campaign which wasn't going anywhere. Bedford, as we have seen never supported the siege or put the weight of his army behind it. By the time Joan came, the English were already losing their grip on Orléans; she just completed the process of wresting it out of their hands. Also, Joan had disagreements with the seasoned warriors and soldiers who accompanied her: she cut an impressive figure in full plate armour, riding a white horse and with a sword that was said to have belonged to Charles Martel but often the practicalities of waging war meant that she butted heads with her fellow commanders. Joan had a reckless streak, and often wanted to just attack rather than being cautious and considering strategy.

Despite this, and even though it wasn't a catastrophic defeat for the English the relief of Orléans did bolster Joan's reputation which was exactly what Charles, and his mother-in-law had intended. Joan was received with riotous celebrations and was lauded as the person who had saved the city and would save her people. Within weeks, Joan was already becoming a legendary figure due to careful fostering of her reputation. To John, Duke of Bedford the loss of 800 men at Orléans was a costly setback but not an insurmountable one, and Joan was just a French whore who deserved to be treated with contempt. They had called her a trollop and a witch: and as far as the English were concerned, she'd just been lucky at Orléans, but she was about to prove how much of a problem she could be.

After she had proved her divine mission at Orléans, Joan began pestering the dauphin to go to Rheims to be crowned. Although he was grateful and had composed a letter on 9 May to tell people in far way Languedoc of her achievements, he wasn't about to allow himself to be ordered around by a teenage girl, heavenly vison or no. He also refused to personally lead the French army, giving that instead to the duke of Alençon. Alençon was only a few years older that Joan and in hindsight, he was probably a very bad choice to entrust her to the care and command of, because he was very keen on astrology and necromancy. Joan doesn't seem to have had an issue with either and she was able to wrap the young Alençon around her little finger.

It wasn't until June 1429 that Joan led another military expedition. This time it was her turn to lay siege to a town. That town was Jargeau, only 11 miles away from Orléans. Joan arrived on the eleventh of June and again sent a missive telling the English to surrender. Jargeau was held by the earl of Suffolk, who had just barely got away from Orléans. Joan quickly found out, despite her initial bravado that sieges were not quick affairs and when rumours came of a relief army headed for Jargeau under the leadership of the experienced Sir John Fastolf, she apparently pressed for an immediate attack. Jargeau is where one of the most controversial actions of Joan's career appears to have taken place. Although it is an incident which is not often publicised because it somewhat tarnishes her saintly reputation. Suffolk, it appears had approached the French with a view to negotiating a surrender twice during the siege which lasted only four days. The first time, his approaches were ignored and the second time, Alençon claimed that he had not heard. Or was it more the case that Joan did not want a negotiated surrender and instead wanted to take the town by storming the English fortifications as had happened at Orléans? That was exactly what happened: the French attacked with scaling ladders, and hacked away at the defenders for several hours before they finally gave way. Suffolk himself surrendered, and one of his brothers by the name of Alexander was killed.

The casualty rate at Jargeau was unusually high: and Juliet Barker has suggested there may have been killing of most of the garrison who may have surrendered after the battle.[4] Such an event, if it truly happened would have been the medieval equivalent of a war crime as was the refusal to countenance a negotiated handover beforehand. Joan as a person of common stock may not have been burdened by the expectations of the code of chivalry which nobles were, and considering how Alençon seems to have been so smitten with Joan he may have simply gone along with it. Following Jargeau, Joan and the army went along besieging some other Loire towns for the next few days, until they were greeted by the unexpected sight of Arthur de Richemont with a thousand or so troops at his command.

As a result of his continual vacillation between the French and English, Richemont had been exiled by Charles and denied permission to take part in any kind of military engagement. Nevertheless, Joan and her fellow commanders went out to meet him and accepted him: its possible that Richemont's timely entry into events was also orchestrated by Yolande of Aragon. His arrival of his army caused the captain of the town of Meung lost his nerve and agreed to a negotiated surrender on the eighteenth of June. The English garrison left heading for Paris and were harassed by the French as they went. Now several French towns had been lost to the French in two months, Joan was considered more of a serious threat. Yet John still didn't engage with her in person: he was more interested in trying to ensure that the Anglo-Burgundian alliance was shored up and staying out of the Loire Valley.

He had sent John Fastolf and several other captains with an army to deal with Joan and Alençon. They finally arrived shortly after the English garrison left Meung on 18 June. In fact, they arrived at a small village called Patay some 15 miles away from Orléans. There they found out their enemies were in hot pursuit. The English were going to adopt their usual strategy of a barrage of arrows, but the archers under the command of John Talbot, Earl of Shrewsbury weren't able to drive their protective stakes into the ground, or they may have been forced to move away from a defensive position and didn't have time to properly get organised before the vanguard of the French cavalry crashed into the ranks of the English archers. In the ensuing slaughter, over 2,000 men were killed among the English, and several of the commanders were captured including Talbot. Fastolf, though, managed to escape with some of his soldiers who tried to flee to the nearby town of Janville, only to find the gates had been closed against them and ended up having to travel some 40 miles to take refuge at the town of Étampes.

The victory at Patay is sometimes attributed to Joan, but it was really one of her commanders who was behind it. The man who had commanded the vanguard who had mown down Talbot's archers was called Étienne de Vignolles, also known as La Hire. It was also due as much to English disorganisation as anything else: one source asserts that Talbot had hidden his archers to take the French by surprise, but their position had been betrayed by a stag which ran out of the bushes. The French, hearing the cheers at seeing the animal (considered a sign of good luck) realised where they were. When John received word of the defeat the next day from Fastolf himself, he was furious and had Fastolf divested of his position as a Knight of the Garter: some dubbed him a coward for having run away from the battle. However, John eventually realised that Fastolf had saved a good proportion of his troops and had that the defeat was more due to the over-confidence of the other commanders than to him. Within a few months, Fastolf had his position restored and John appointed him as Lieutenant of Caen.[5]

John was then stationed at Corbeil. This was the town to which his dying brother had been carried in 1422, and there for the first time John seems to have seriously considered the threat of the French teenager who had bedevilled the English for the last several months. John, of course, did not believe that she was sent from heaven: that would have meant admitting the cause he had devoted the better part of a decade of his life to was wrong. He thought, like many among the English that she was a witch, and even wrote to the council calling her a 'disciple and limb of the fiend' that is of the devil or of demons.[6] When rumours began to reach him, however that Joan intended to storm Paris John did not let himself be influenced by superstition and started to take practical steps to protect shore up the city's defences. The walls were strengthened, and guns deposited on the walls. John also made sure that someone was on watch on the walls of the city 24 hours a day and petitioned the council in England to send reinforcements without any delay. He wasn't about the lose the capital city which the English had fought so long and so hard to capture to an upstart French witch and her attack dogs.

Buoyed by their recent victories the dauphin finally decided to go into action and take to the field himself: instead of marching to battle, however, at the goading of Joan he decided to march instead to Reims for his coronation in a triumphal progress. All were to know that their rightful king was to be restored to them. In this, he ignored the advice of his counsellors who urged him to make war on Normandy. Joan took it upon herself to summon all good and loyal Frenchmen to attend, and as they marched only Troyes held out. On 16 July he was received with honour by crowds in Reims and then crowned the following day by the archbishop of Reims. There had been a Burgundian garrison in the city, but they had withdrawn ahead of the advance of the dauphin and Joan, essentially ceding control of the city to them. Reims was not, of course, the traditional site for the coronation of French kings: that was Paris but since that city was still under English control there was no chance of doing it there without taking the city first. There was, however, one precedent. Clovis, a fifth-century Frankish king and founder of the Merovingian dynasty had been crowned there by another archbishop of Reims nearly a thousand years earlier.

The French king couldn't use the traditional regalia because that too was in the hands of the English, but Joan's standard was placed near the high altar of the church. Nevertheless, Charles and others may have felt somewhat short-changed at having to rehash a millennia old ceremony instead of being crowned at the place where his father and grandfather had been. Nevertheless, the people were elated, and many greeted him as King Charles VII and took what had happened as further proof that Joan was indeed being guided by the hand of God.

Joan's parents attended the ceremony – but there were several notable absentees including the duke of Burgundy. Joan wrote a letter to him, chastising him for not being there, but her tone was rather more polite and conciliatory than her other missives. Charles was still trying to win over Burgundy because, despite the dreams of Joan and his advisors, he realised that there was no hope of a long-term victory or to permanently expel the English without Burgundian support. Burgundy was, instead, in Paris where had arrived on 10 July was received by his brother-in-law Bedford and his sister. Anne welcomed him and may well have been responsible for him staying there a week. The two men had quarrelled at the last meeting in April. However, as always, Burgundy was hedging his bets, and he sent an envoy with congratulations for Charles.

In Paris, at a special church service everyone present was reminded of how the duke's father had been treacherously murdered by Charles and his adherents – it was a move designed to stir up hatred about the Armagnacs among those who might have some residual sympathy for them. In Corbiel, John also made a will in which he left a large portion of his lands and also another curious bequest: that his executors were to hand over all his goods and furniture to Anne 'for the services she had rendered' to her husband. It was normal for husbands to leave bequests to their wives but what John was doing here is interesting. What were these 'services' Anne had rendered? He was speaking about her like she was member of his household and a trusted servant as well as his wife. These will be explained later, but they may very well have involved Anne spying on her brother.

After the grand gesture of his meeting with his brother-in-law, John lambasted the crowd present in Paris for having been outmanoeuvred by Charles and his witch. He reminded them that was his nephew, Henry to whom they owed their allegiance, and he was the one who should have been crowned, not Charles. He wrote the council in England asking that they arrange his coronation as king of France as quickly as possible and send further reinforcements. For years, Bedford had been struggling to secure money and men for the continuing war in France and in the late 1420s he was having to rely more and more on foreign troops or the men of English garrisons. On the 25 July, John finally got his reinforcements: some 2,700 men led by none other than his uncle, Cardinal Henry Beaufort. Beaufort had only given him the army because he felt guilty; the troops had been raised by Beaufort himself for a crusade against a group called the Hussites in Bohemia, a territory in what is now the Czech Republic. They were another 'heretical' sect who had their roots in the English Lollards, but when the council had received John's letter begging for help and the news of Joan's victories the army was hastily redirected to France.

With his reinforcements, John began to prepare to defend Paris. It was very much a case of when you want something done properly, do it yourself for him. He would entrust the task to nobody else and delegate it to nobody else. First, he went to Montereau where he issued a challenge to Charles to come to Paris and take him on. John's act of bravado was probably measured to hide the fact that, despite their meetings and propaganda efforts, the alliance with Burgundy was still faltering. John began to fudge things, he wrote a letter to the council in the first week of August telling them the alliance was a strong and before, when Burgundy was entertaining none other than the archbishop of Reims at his palace in Arras. His wife, Anne had been sent there as a spy to keep an eye on her brother's movements and was constantly feeding information back to her husband in Paris. As in his youth, John was still making use of spies, only this time it was his wife, and she was apparently a willing participant. It shows something of the relationship between them that Anne was willing to spy on her brother at the behest of her husband. At about this time, John started to refer to the late duke of Burgundy, Philip and Anne's father as *his* father too. In his challenge to Charles, he couched the newly styled king of France's murder of John the Fearless a decade earlier as an offense against himself, not just against the duke of Burgundy. What he did was a further attempt to win over the vacillating Burgundy by showing him that John was dedicated to his family and its continued unity.

Second, John reminded the people of Paris of the perfidy and treachery for Charles and his party, who had a 'sluttish' and unnatural woman in their ranks as well as an apostate friar. Rumours had already begun to fly that Alençon and Joan were lovers, rumours which John probably hoped to capitalise on as well as the fact that she had been joined by a friar who had been thrown out of Paris for his conduct. John's propaganda worked: although the people of Paris still also had horrible memories of the sack of the city in 1418 by the Burgundians and their knowledge of what a vengeful invading army could do.

Charles and Joan took John's bait. By 14 August Joan and several of Charles commanders arrived outside Paris with a large army. That August was blisteringly and unseasonably hot and as the sun reflected off the armour of the French army, it must have been an imposing sight. Yet once again, Charles himself was not there. Even though he had newly been crowned he did not take personal command of his army, leaving it to others and relying on Joan as a figurehead. There the two armies waited: and waited for a battle. Yet not battle came. Instead, there was a war of attrition with sorties and skirmishes. Any movement of soldiers reportedly kicked up so much dirt and dust from the parched ground that it was hard to tell which side was which. The days dragged on, and still very little happened. The English were not going to budge an inch or lose ground again. Bedford's careful planning and organisation held strong once again. Even though the main body of his army was not in Paris, and he was waiting at Senlis nearby his forces within the city held firm.

Joan, in her typical teenage impetuosity was the first person to give in. She rode near to the English lines with her banner and dared them to come out and fight her. Her provocation didn't work. The English had learned from Orléans; Jargeau and Patay did not engage her when she threatened them. When her challenge didn't work, she tried to be more polite and diplomatic. She sent a message to the English telling them that Charles awaited them and would fight them when they were ready. Their only response was to totally ignore her. Joan, it seemed, had lost most of her capacity to scare or overawe her adversaries. The novelty was wearing off.

A few days after their arrival, the French heard that John and the English army were headed to Paris. Before he was able to get there though, he had to delay his plans to deal with wider problems in Normandy: several places within the Duchy, upon hearing of Charles coronation and the approach of his army had capitulated or were threatening to submit to him. John was not willing to allow Normandy to topple when he'd taken care to ensure Paris was prepped for a long siege. Although he was by then 40 years of age, John had apparently lost none of his vigour and energy. He still took sudden changes of plan and emergencies in his stride, responding promptly and doing whatever he could to ensure they were resolved. He took up a strategic position at Vernon in between Rouen and Paris and sent relief to the town of Évreux which was being threatened by Armagnac troops. At Vernon, Bedford summoned all the troops that he possibly could, took out loans from his uncle and even pawned some of his jewellery to ensure that wages were paid. He was able to rescue some of the threatened towns for the time being, but Charles offensive had two fronts. In Arras, he was making moves to try to reconcile the duke of Burgundy with all kinds of compromises and in the end John's invocation of the name of his murdered father had the desired effect.

Philippe was still not quite prepared to come to terms with Charles, but he did make a four-month truce with him, agreeing not to engage in hostilities in or around Paris in case Charles was able to take the city for himself. Joan and her fellow warriors, meanwhile had to content themselves with attacking the suburbs of Paris. On 26 August, they took St Denis, but this was hardly a glorious victory since the garrison and most of the inhabitants had already left for the safety of Paris. They basically walked into a half-empty settlement and were able to claim it because nobody was left to fight them. As August turned into September, John finally set a date return to Paris with all the troops he could muster, and the defences of Normandy shored up for the time being. In an attempt to pre-empt him on the eighth day of September Joan once again rode up the to gates with her banner and demanded her enemies surrender the city. Thereafter followed an exchange of fire from canons, and an attack was made upon the walls, but it was hopeless and nobody within the city was prepared to open the gates to Joan or her Armagnac allies.

Joan's favourite tactic was to fight under her personal standard in the defensive ditches near cities and after a long day of fighting with the defenders outside Paris she stood in a ditch once more and called on the defenders to surrender yelling that if they did not let her into the city before nightfall she and the Armagnacs would break in and kill everyone without mercy. It was an empty threat, and the English knew it. Reportedly one English solider on the walls yelled back a defiant response and called her a 'bloody tart' before shooting his crossbow at her.[7] The crossbow bolt struck her in the thigh, and another one struck her standard bearer in his foot, pinning him to the ground. Then a second hit him squarely in the skull between his eyes, killing him instantly and taking down Joan's sacred banner with it.

For the first time since her debut five months earlier, Joan's presence did not inspire her troops to keep on attacking. Though she tried and tried to rally them to continue the attack, all she succeeded in doing was bleeding out into the mud of a Parisian trench and shouting herself hoarse whilst her standard lay on the ground at her feet. God, it seemed, was no longer listening to His servant and didn't seem inclined to grant her another miracle. In a final humiliation Joan had to be dragged from the trench as the trumpets were sounded for the Armagnac army to retreat. As they rescued their hero, the canons ceased to fire, and the Armagnac forces withdrew from the walls of Paris. Before John had even returned to Paris, he had managed to do what none of the other English commanders had: enable his men to hold out against the legendary Joan of Arc and, in the process, demonstrate that she was not invincible. When he heard what had happened, John must have privately thanked God and felt vindicated in his belief that this French sorceress was a mere flash in the pan who was already losing credibility in the sight of both the English and the French. When he finally returned to the city two days after the Charles withdrawal on 11 September, he publicly gave thanks in the cathedral of Notre Dame and laid a gold coin at the altar. He also levied a hefty fine on the people of St Denis for having abandoned the place allowing Joan to basically walk in unchallenged.

Deep down John knew that he'd had a narrow escape. Although he made much at having saved Paris and had taken down France's darling a peg or two in the process, it had been a close call. The coronation of Charles had been a great propaganda victory and was encouraging many in France to rebel against English authority: something which had been unthinkable for years. His resources were also strained to near breaking point, even with his uncle's army. If his own spin campaign had failed and Charles or Joan had been able to win the hearts and minds of the Parisians things could have gone very differently. For this reason, at the end of September John took the gamble of appointing Burgundy the governor of Paris. By this time, of course, his truce with Charles had ended and John had made certain that there were no more negotiations which he did not know about or did not have representatives present at. Burgundy was again greeted with honour in Paris, where John was also reunited with his wife.

It was unusual for the wife of a duke to go and stay with her birth relatives for prolonged periods, as Anne did. Her absence, during which time she had been with her brother seems to have been entirely John's idea because he needed someone to act as eyes and ears in Burgundy's court. It has already been demonstrated that she was spying for him because her position made her the ideal candidate to do so. Whether or not Phillippe of Burgundy knew what his sister was up to is another matter. He may have trusted her so much that he never suspected a thing, or just turned a blind eye because of the affection he held for her. Either way, he now had the position of the governor of Paris as a sweetener. On 15 October, before a meeting of the council of France, Bedford went a step further and appointed his brother-in-law as lieutenant-governor of all the English possessions in France except for Normandy. Privately, he discussed the possibility of a counter-attack on Charles because the appointment had a double purpose. It was intended to remind Burgundy that John still trusted him but also to ensure he realised that he was expected main loyal to England. John had given him both positions, and he could take then away if Burgundy didn't toe the line.

Aftermath and a Coronation

Meanwhile, Joan had limped back to Charles lands in the Loire where she may have begun to question her mission. Or simply have blamed Charles for not continuing the assault on Paris. In November, John's plans began to come to fruition. On 8 November 1429, Henry VI was crowned king of England at Westminster Abbey. He wasn't yet 8 years old, and his coronation had been pushed forward by several months if not a couple of years. The event was a direct response to Charles coronation because Bedford was already planning for the young king to cross the Channel and be crowned king of France.

In January 1430, John also attended the marriage of Philippe of Burgundy to Isabella of Portugal. Isabella was the granddaughter of John of Gaunt. Her mother had been the sister of King Henry IV and so she was John's first cousin. Although it was unlikely that they'd met before 1430, his brother had once considered Isabella as a bride, not apparently concerned about the close blood relationship between them. Philippe had already buried two wives by 1430, both of whom had been connected to the Armagnacs in some way, and this third marriage was clearly a measured attempt to strengthen his alliance with England. In early March of the following year John gave his brother-in-law the counties of Champagne and Brie. These were to be held by Philippe as a vassal of King Henry VI. John wasn't just trying to shore up the Anglo-Burgundian alliance: he was also reminding Burgundy of what it really meant. Burgundy had once sworn allegiance to his brother Henry V, accepting him as king of France and his feudal lord. That allegiance was now transferred to the son and heir of his late brother as was the natural order of things with medieval kingship. Burgundy held his new lands from King Henry, not from the man who called himself King Charles VII. This wasn't just an abstract idea: if the duke of Burgundy was to swear fealty to or submit to Charles after Henry was crowned in France, he could be held guilty of treason. The same applied to any in France who were officially aligned with Burgundy and with England. These gifts of land were also intended as an incentive to encourage Philippe to reclaim Troyes and Reims which had pledged themselves to Charles the previous year.

The people of Reims were so concerned that they wrote a letter to Joan of Arc begging her to come to their aid. Joan of Arc had gone back to fighting, but on a smaller scale and this time she had to beg and rely on the goodwill of others to raise men and money for the fight. Although Charles still officially favoured her and even ennobled her and her family in December 1430, he was no longer giving her his blessing for military expeditions except a punitive expedition against a minor mercenary captain in the Loire. When she received the message from Reims in the spring of 1431, she sent an encouraging response, but her hands were tied, and she was not able to do anything because she and Charles had gone back to his lands in the Loire more than a hundred miles away and protecting the newly submitted cities and towns didn't seem to be high on Charles list of priorities.

In late April, Henry VI landed at Calais for his coronation as king of France. John hoped that his nephew would bring a fresh army with him comparable in size to the invasion force that his father had brought to France for the Battle of Agincourt some fifteen years earlier and he delivered. Just before he arrived, an army of over 3,000 men crossed the Channel. They were placed under the command of one John, the bastard of Clarence. This man was the illegitimate son of none other than Thomas, Duke of Clarence and the cousin of King Henry VI. A further army of nearly 5,000 were commissioned to come with the king himself. To fund this army, the Lords had to approve huge grants of taxation, and many nobles were expected to cough up to raise troops from their own estates to contribute to the royal army. Twenty-two nobles accompanied Henry to France, including his 18-year-old cousin, Richard, Duke of York. Richard was the heir of the duke of York who had perished at Agincourt, but not his son. He was instead his nephew – Richard's father was the earl of Cambridge who had been executed only a few weeks before Agincourt. Nobody then could have predicted the future bitter rivalry between Henry and Richard and their adherents which would later tear England apart and claim the lives of most of the royal family. The young Henry VI was supposed to have made a grand royal progress to Paris, accompanied by the flower of the English nobility and his army to be crowned king, and then nominally preside over a campaign to regain all the territory which had been lost since 1429. He wouldn't have led the army himself, of course. He was only 8.

That at least was the plan. What actually happened was that when Henry arrived at Calais, he had to remain there for several months because the truces between the English, Burgundians and Armagnacs had expired a week earlier. The king's safety could not be guaranteed if he had to travel through territory that might be beset by enemy soldiers or bandits, and so he settled down and stayed in Calais. The duke of Burgundy finally decided to reclaim some of the lands which had been granted to him in late March, and began marching through Armagnac territory headed, apparently headed for Compiègne. Joan saw her opportunity to get back into the field. She had effectively been unemployed and side-lined by Charles for five months and so she seized that opportunity. She left the Loire accompanied by some of her loyal captains, her brother Pierre, and 200 or so men and headed for a city which she believed would soon be under siege by the Burgundians. Her intention was to re-enact what she had done at Orléans, but this time she did not have Charles blessing. She left the court and took her men with her without royal permission because she was tired of being left out of the action. What Joan did wasn't just reckless, it was potentially treasonable: royal vassals were not supposed to leave the court without the permission of the king and take private armies with them. She seems to have been relying on her good reputation and her run of victories the previous year to get away with it. She hoped of course to achieve another triumph and prove herself useful again, but her luck was about to run out.

Joan and her troops managed to get to Soissons, but when they arrived, they were not warmly received. Armagnac loyalists were no longer welcome because the duke of Burgundy and his men were already there. Joan was allowed a bed for the night, but her men were forced to stay outside the town. Her plans had to change, and Joan was search for reinforcements before sneaking into Compiègne under cover of darkness. The following day, on realizing the siege had tightened she and some of her men decided to make a sortie out of the town to try and attack the Burgundians. On the day of 22 or 23 May, Joan's military career ended when she was captured during the same sortie. It appears that she was caught between two armies and simply outnumbered by her enemies and so had no choice but to surrender.

Some modern movies and other commentators claim that Joan was captured by treachery, but there's no evidence for this. What seems to have taken place is that towards the evening, the gate was opened to let Joan and her men out, to gallop across the bridge and drive a portion of the Burgundian army back towards their camp twice. As they wheeled back and charged their enemies for the third time, a division of English troops who had been kept back intercepted her. She and her men attempted to retreat across some fields but some of the Burgundians, realizing who they were dealing with, surrounded her and pulled her from her horse. The rumours about a betrayal might have come from the fact that when her troops were trying to retreat with their enemies in hot pursuit that the captain of Compiègne, fearing enemy soldiers would soon start pouring in decided to close the gates. Realistically, he had no choice. Nevertheless, many soon started to play the blame game and attribute malicious motives to the closing of the gate on the retreating Joan and her men which resulted in her captured and the deaths of some 400 of her troops.

The truth is that Joan simply seems to have over-reached herself and relied too much on her divine mission for success rather than realizing she had been outnumbered and outmatched. For all her reputation and her saintly aura, Joan of Arc was at the end of the day an 18-year-old girl with barely a year of military experience behind her. Unlike John of Bedford, Henry V or Philippe of Burgundy who had been raised to fight and acquainted with the ways of war before they were even teenagers, Joan had lived the life of a commoner.

She'd never had a great head for strategy, generally leaving that to her fellow commanders and favoured direct tactics: attacking and then pressing forward the attack until God helped her overcome her enemies. It had worked a few times, and Joan's man problem seems to have been that she didn't learn her lesson when charging and encouraging her men to continue fighting against a much stronger foe in the name of God had failed for the first time at Paris. Some might say that Joan's outlook was that of a fanatic or a zealot in the sense that Joan was so assured of her divine destiny that she simply didn't know when she was beaten and refused to give up. There may be some truth in this claim: what some would see as determination occasionally proved to be a stubborn hot-headedness about Joan in which she asked her soldiers to keep fighting in impossible situations when they could see victory was impossible – such as in the trenches before the walls of Paris the year before.

One other possible reason why Joan was captured was because she stuck out like a proverbial sore thumb; not just because of her banner, but also because of her clothing. Joan had taken to wearing rich robes and ostentatious outfits. When captured, she was wearing scarlet and gold robes over armour which was designed to look pure white and shine in the sun.[8] No more was she the humble peasant girl: she'd taken to dressing this way to fit in with the nobles around her, and, of course, now deemed herself noble. Her white armour was probably intended as a visual symbol of her purity and godliness, yet all this and her robes served to do in the end was make her more of a target.

Joan surrendered herself to the Burgundians (she didn't trust the English, presumably), and was given into the care of Jean de Luxembourg who was allied with the Burgundians and whose soldiers she had attacked during the sortie. News spread quickly about the capture of the woman who had been the Burgundians most feared opponent for the better part of a year. The duke of Burgundy himself seems to have learned of it within a day, and dispatched missives to all the great and good among his allies. To him it was evidence that Joan's mission had never been divinely ordained. The Armagnacs too began to circulate the news. Their interpretation was that Joan had been captured because she was too wilful and stubborn, refusing to listen to good advice from her elders and superiors. Three days after her capture the scholars of the University of Paris, one of the foremost theological institutions of medieval Christendom, wrote the duke of Burgundy asking that she be turned over to them to interrogate her on suspicion of possible heresy. Contrary to what history tells us though, John, Duke of Bedford had nothing to do with this part of the process, nor any particular interest in it. He was probably glad Joan had been captured but he had more important things on his mind. Most notably, his own future.

Chapter Eleven

A New King of France

In October 1429, following their meeting after the city had been attacked, Philippe and Bedford both left Normandy. For John, it was a permanent relocation. He had lived and made his headquarters in Paris for much of his time as regent, but decided to up sticks and move to Rouen, the capital of Normandy. John took his entire library to Rouen with him: a precious collection which he had spent many years collecting and was not, of course, going to leave behind. They included the famous and previously mentioned Bedford Hours, as well as a psalter and a personal prayer book. It also included a popular work of religious devotion called *The Pilgrimage of the Soul*. Bedford's copy was not in English but was a translation from the original French into Latin. Some of the books he'd obtained from his late brother, others were his own acquisitions. In Paris, John had even employed his own librarian to take care of his and his wife's precious collection of books, but he had to let the man go when he moved.

Bedford established himself not in a castle or one of the cities great fortresses, but allegedly in a house near the port St Hilaire. Rouen proved to be a city which was very close to Bedford's heart. He established good relationships with local merchants and tried his best to serve the interests of the citizens. In October 1430, Bedford managed to achieve his ambition to be admitted to the fraternity of the canons of Rouen Cathedral. One might ask how a person who wasn't a member of the clergy could enter a religious order without becoming a monk or priest. He was able to enter the fraternity because they were what was known as secular canons. Men who lived together in the style of a religious order but had not taken the vows which monks did. John could not afford to take vows, because he was still married to Anne and still hoped for an heir and so he it was the perfect fraternity to enter. The ceremony involved being invested with the robes of the canons of the Order, and then swearing on a copy the gospels up uphold the rights and liberties of the church. The account of his investiture mentioned that John had recently been laid low with an illness from which he had not yet fully recovered. We don't know what the illness was, but it was severe enough to be debilitating and seems to have afflicted him at times of great stress. In April of that year, John he had been deprived of the title of regent and most of his lands.

Afterwards, John set about trying to establish two religious houses in Rouen. His brother Henry had established a monastic house near London and his sister, Philippa had also established one in Sweden. John wanted to do one better: literally, by establishing two. First, he commissioned at monastery for an order known as the Celestines, an offshoot of the Benedictines to whom his wife had a special devotion. He acquired some land near his own house for the project, although building was very slow and was not completed before his death. Secondly, he established a monastery for an order called the Carmelites who had already lost their monastery situated outside the walls of Rouen due to the war. His gifts of money and tithes to the Carmelites were eventually used by them to pay for masses to be said for John and his wife. John's foundations happened when, for the first time in years he had time on his hands.

Henry VI in France

From the moment Henry VI landed in France in April 1430, John's career was put in jeopardy. Cardinal Beaufort had drawn up a series of ordinances before Henry even left England: they asked for a radical shakeup of the government in the parts of France ruled by the House of Lancaster. John's 'title and power as Regent were to be suspended'.[1] Instead of John, all decisions were to be made by a council consisting of a group of men who were confidents of the king. John hadn't been fired, but he had as good as been. Of course, he would have known that his tenure as regent of France would end as soon as Henry VI came of age but he had not expected to be replaced as soon as his young nephew landed, nor to find out the whole thing had been planned by the uncle whom he previously trusted.

By removing his powers from him, the council were basically saying he had failed, and they no longer trusted him to competently exercise authority in France. The rule of the Anglo-French realm had been based on the understanding that John needed to have the power to conduct the war where and when he wanted, in the manner he wanted. He also needed to have the flexibility to raise the money and resources he needed.[2] This power had now effectively been usurped by being handed over to people who didn't have the experience or knowledge necessary.

It was more than a slap on the face. It was saying that everything John had done in the last eight years, the victory he had won at Verneuil and all the years he poured his blood, sweat and tears into preserving England's interests had been for nothing. Then, just to add insult to injury, John was stripped of his most valuable lands and lordships which were the source of most of his revenues. He was being treated like not just a failure, but a criminal. John fell out with his uncle because of what happened, and it is likely that he never forgave him. The English discussed replacing John as a commander with, among others, the illegitimate son of his brother the duke of Clarence whose career in France had been unremarkable until his death. This plan though was soon abandoned, and they opted for a strategy proposed by the Burgundians in meetings which John was largely absent from.

1430 was John's *annus horriblus*, and it wasn't about to improve. Retiring to Rouen, John had months to spend on his religious projects and await the coronation of the young king whilst his noble peers spoke about reclaiming all the lands which had been lost in 1429. Yet even whilst they boasted, things went badly for them. In October, the Anglo-Burgundian siege of Compiègne failed, due in a large part to English desertions because soldiers were not receiving their pay, which led to a disagreement between their commanders, the earl of Huntingdon and Jean de Luxembourg and recriminations all around. Philippe of Burgundy blamed the English for what had happened and wrote a series of angry letters to Henry VI's council. He complained of not having been paid, of Armagnac troops ravaging his lands, and of the capture of four members of his household. This stands in some contrast to what had happened when John was in control: he had always somehow been able to find money, even if he had to take out loans or pawn his valuables. Philippe also complained about the whole course which the war was taking and the financial burden which had been placed on him. He'd never complained about costs when he was campaigning alongside John, but again that was because Bedford was adept at paying for his own troops or raising them from English lands – and probably because he was used to campaigning with his brother-in-law rather than the new council with whom he had to trash out policy. In truth, Beaufort's policies were probably to blame for what happened: Beaufort changed the system so that pay went to individual soldiers rather than to the captains to distribute among them. Beaufort also appointed many of the men who had come over with the king in 1429 as captains, which caused resentment among those who had been in Normandy for years and served alongside Bedford or Salisbury. It wasn't just personal preference, but instead a matter of experience and the relationships which these captains had forged over years, as well as John's involvement in government and his knowledge of what worked best in the Norman lands which had worked so well.[3]

All the while Phillip was campaigning and John of Bedford was establishing churches, Joan of Arc's future was being decided. It was French clerics began to shout about heresy mere days after her capture. The vicar-general of Paris, who was under the auspices of the Inquisition had written to the duke of Burgundy saying that she smelled of heresy and then the University of Paris suggested she be tried in Paris. Henry V's council supported her trial but just not in Paris because it was too prominent. The English felt that her trial for heresy would help to discredit her claim to have been sent by God and deprive her of the moral impact of her victories. It was for this reason that the English became interested in obtaining her: but the timing of the everything that took place shows one thing. John, coronation of Bedford was not person behind the decision that she be tried, and he was not the person who paid Jean de Luxembourg who she was in the charge of. Pierre Cauchon was put in charge of the trail against her, and he was a close friend of the duke of Bedford, but so were many others. The man who raised the vast sum of 120,000 *livres* to pay Jean for Joan's person was in fact Cardinal Beaufort. Modern commentators and filmmakers who blame John for what happened to Joan because he was regent of France are, once again, looking in the wrong place and have their facts misplaced.

When Joan heard that she was to be handed over to the English she thew herself off the top of a castle tower into a dry moat and was badly injured. Two days before Christmas in 1430, she was taken to Rouen and put into the custody of the earl of Warwick who lodged her in one Rouen's castles (there were then at least two). This was probably the closest she ever came to Bedford: being housed in the same city as him at the time when he was living there. John though wasn't really all that interested in Joan. He was quite happy to allow his friend Cauchon and the church to do its job.

In early January 1431, when Joan's trial began all the leading figures involved were Burgundians who had a political stake in her conviction and the church who had a religious stake in it. Her trial began in January and lasted for months. The conclusion was perhaps not as inevitable as we are apt to think. Although inquisitors were involved in Joan's trial, they did not always find people guilty of heresy. But so many political forces were invested in the trial that it was very unlikely Joan would ever have been acquitted. Yet on 9 May, when the church's protected trial was at an end and Joan had been a captive for nearly a year, something unexpected happened. Beset by ill health, and sorely pressed for weeks by those who interrogated her, Joan submitted to the church and said that her visions had been false. She recanted. This meant that Cauchon could not sentence her to death. Heretics who recanted had to be forgiven and accepted back into the fold of the church. Yet the church was not willing to simply let Joan go to return home to her village nor to Charles, so she was instead sentenced to life imprisonment. Later in her cell, Joan removed the doublet and hose: the men's clothing that she had worn for so long and donned instead a woman's dress. Her hair, which had grown long in the interval of her imprisonment, was also shaved. If things had remained in this way, despite being sentenced to imprisonment, Joan of Arc could have won. Her military career had ended a year earlier and there would be no chance to return to it, but she had denied Cauchon and the duke of Burgundy their chance to kill the 'Armagnac whore'.[4] On the day of the 28 May, however, Cauchon was called back to Joan's cell.

There they found Joan in great distress and discovered she had, once again, put on her male attire. When asked why she had done so after swearing not to, she said she did not realise that she'd sworn any such oath and, besides, it was more convenient to dress in male attire when she was forced to live among men. She wore it for her own protection to prevent herself being harassed. Furthermore, Joan then said Cauchon had not held up his side of the bargain. She claimed that she had been told she'd be allowed to go to mass if she submitted and she wanted to be sent to a place where she could live among women. If she got that, then she'd go back to doing what her judges had told her. Cauchon then took council from other clerics, but they concluded that Joan had relapsed back into her heretical ways. There was only one sentence for a relapsed heretic: death. The day after 29 May they sent another judge, Pierre Maurice to see her. He informed her that her death was assured because she was relapsed, but that there was still a chance to save her soul. He asked her about he point on which her condemnation had hinged: were her visions and the voices she had heard real or were they not? Joan asserted that she didn't know if she had heard from good or evil spirits, but that yes, her voices were real. They had spoken to her: especially during the ringing of church bells for Matins. What's more angels had appeared to her many times and in many forms, as she had asserted at her trial. The angel she claimed to have seen at Charles' trial who had carried his crown, however, was not real. That angel had been herself. At that moment, Cauchon came in once again and asked her had her voices not told her she would be released? They had, admitted Joan and she had been deceived. Yet no last-minute submission could save Joan this time: her fate had been decided the day before. After being given the eucharist, she was put on a cart which trundled through the crowed streets to the market square of Rouen. There she was helped up a scaffold which had already been erected and tied to the stake by English soldiers after the charges against her were once again repeated. The fire was lit, and as it began to rise around her, Joan was heard to cry out 'Jesus' three times. She was 19 years old.

One question that begs posing here whether Charles could have done more to save his heavenly maid who had allowed him to be crowned king. He could have raised the money to pay Jean de Luxembourg, but its likely he didn't want to upset the Burgundians by ransoming her which is what she might have hoped. Once she was in the hands of the church, any attempt by Charles to save her would also have become more difficult as he could not afford to upset the University of Paris or the church. People were already saying that her visions were from the devil rather than from God and he was tainted by that association. Charles did not want to risk saving a woman who might be deemed a heretic because it would reflect so badly on him.

John, Duke of Bedford was not in Rouen on the day of Joan's execution. He had travelled to Paris in late January. His only real involvement was that his wife Anne had supervised another test of Joan's virginity, but then she went to Paris as well. John took with him to the capital seventy barges full of supplies for the beleaguered city. He had got them past any Armagnac bandits ravaging the countryside by having them sailed along the river Seine. John was greeted as a hero by the people of Paris, coming once again to their aid and preceding the arrival of the young Henry whose coronation was eagerly anticipated. John was happy to leave Joan's trial in the hands of his uncle Cardinal Beaufort in Rouen. In fact, he was probably glad to see the back of him. It wasn't until early June that he heard of the fate of Joan, and then sent missives to other parts of Christendom about it. Sermons were preached, denouncing her and her heresy and Charles, very wisely kept his mouth shut. He still had his supporters, including the archbishop of Reims who reminded others that he was still an anointed king, Joan notwithstanding. Nothing could undo that or remove God's blessing from him. However, his power base was beset by chaos and infighting among his nobles which Joan of Arc had done very little to end this. In October, the English were able to retake the city of Louviers between Rouen and Paris was retaken by the English. It had fallen to La Hire more than a year earlier. The mighty Château Gaillard, an ancient fortress which had once belonged to Richard the Lionheart was also back in English hands. The recapture of Louviers cleared the path to Paris.

On 2 December, Henry VI finally made it to the capital for his long-expected coronation. He'd been in France for more than eighteen months by this point and finally was able to do what he had come for. On 16 December, not long after his tenth birthday Henry VI was crowned king of France in Notre Dame cathedral. This was the culmination of everything John, Duke of Bedford had worked for over the last eight years. On the occasion of Henry's coronation, his wife Anne gifted Henry the fine illuminated manuscript which her husband had given her as a wedding present seven years before. This was the Bedford Hours and is one of the reasons why it remains in England to this day. Cardinal Beaufort presided over the coronation instead of the bishop of Paris. There were also mutterings about the coronation festivities having been badly planned and rushed, the food being terrible, and Henry VI hurrying back to England only ten days after the coronation. He never again returned to France.

There was, however, one bright spot in Henry's return to England: John, Duke of Bedford was reinstated as regent of France. Some would argue a regent was not needed now Henry had been crowned, but the young king would not be able to rule either England or France in his own right until he came of age. Therefore, John was able to keep the title until that time, apart from the hiatus in which Lancastrian France had been ruled by the English regency council. John must have waved his uncle goodbye with a smirk when he went home with Henry in December 1431, because almost as soon as Beaufort was gone, John reversed all the laws and ordinances he had made for the military forces in France. He would go back to doing things his way and using the methods which had worked well for years. However, Bedford was about to learn that he was no longer the charismatic and bold young leader who had stepped into his brother's shoes a decade earlier. He was 43, and the struggles of defending England's conquests in France and keeping a reign on the family members who threatened them had taken their toll. He was used to offensive warfare, but since 1429 England had been on the defensive against an increasingly bold and well-organised enemy. Later, John spoke to his nephew Henry of the events which had transpired in France. Looking back, he thought that England's trouble had begun when the earl of Salisbury died in 1429. Salisbury had been his cousin and one of his closest friends and allies. It was that event which Bedford considered pivotal. Afterwards, he believed the devil had used Joan of Arc to lead his people astray and had begun to work against the interests of the English.

Nobody had ever been able to replace Salisbury, at least as far as Bedford was concerned. Most of the lords and nobles he had known or had come to France with in 1420 were either dead or were like him seasoned veterans. In England, they were becoming relics. The glorious days of Agincourt were waning, and Verneuil too was becoming a distant memory as the political landscape changed around them. In France, some were beginning to resent English presence, and it wasn't just from the usual quarters of Armagnac loyalists. Joan of Arc may not have bene military very successful, but she had awoken something in the French psyche. Furthermore, the duke of Burgundy was becoming increasingly disaffected with England. In May 1431, he threatened that unless the English sent him aid in defending his lands, he would seek other means: referring to a new round of negotiations with Charles of France. Charles was beginning to fear that he had been backing the wrong horse since 1420 and that the future might lie with Charles. In February 1432, one of Roeun's castles had been temporary taken by the French in a daring night assault. A traitor within the castle let them into the courtyard at night, and they scaled the walls using ladders. Interestingly the French had not taken the chance of doing such a thing when Bedford was in the city but had waited until he was away, showing that he could still command a measure of fear and grudging respect: a reputation which he lived up to when the following month, when the men who had taken the castle were forced to surrender, he had 100 of them beheaded in the marketplace. The very same place where Joan had been executed the year before. John had, apparently, initially been in a more merciful mood, and had even offered to give the Frenchmen who held the castle money to leave, but when they refused and forced him to besiege the place for a month, he decided to make an example of them for wasting to much of his time and his resources.

The following month, the French took Chartres, and one of their commanders the Bastard of Orléans (as the name suggests an illegitimate son of one of the dukes) used it as a base for military operations against Paris. They intended to blockade Paris to force it into submission. By the spring of 1432 the grain supplies were already starting to be cut off. Chartres was the first step to a full blockade. The next was capturing Lagny-sur-Marne. In March, the people of Paris wrote to Henry VI to inform him that the town had to be retaken or else 'he would not be the Master of his own Kingdom'.⁵ It was so important that the council of France discussed the matter, and finally retaking the town fell to Bedford. He laid siege to the town for months over the summer of 1432 and drew about 1,500 troops from the garrisons around Normandy and once again asked for reinforcements from England. He struggled to raise an army again, and the numbers he could raise had declined since his uncle and King Henry had taken most of their soldiers home with them. The earl of Arundel's forces were attacked in late May and even the arrival of Bedford himself in early August after several months spent trying to raise men for the siege didn't help matters except as a temporary morale boost. That summer was blisteringly hot and as Bedford settled down for a prolonged siege, but it wasn't too last long.

On 10 August as the garrison were opening negotiations, a small French army was spotted approaching Lagny. Bedford drew up his forces and prepared for a fight: but it was a ruse to draw Bedford's attention away from the town. As the main French army did so, a small division under a Spanish mercenary named Rodrigo de Villandrano went around the English flank with eighty men and more importantly, wagons loaded with supplies. After some fighting around one of the gates, he broke in. The defenders were resupplied, meaning they could hold out even longer against an English siege. With the mission accomplished the main French army withdrew and appeared to be heading for Paris itself. Bedford abandoned the siege and gave chase, believing the capital was threatened, and in his haste abandoned most of his canons and artillery. As soon as he had left the men of Lagny came out and helped themselves to the expensive artillery and took it into the town with them. Bedford was thus humiliated and forced to abandon the siege.

It was the first major setback Bedford had suffered in years and meant the blockade of Paris was strengthened. Worse still, the full wrath of the people of Paris came down upon Bedford who was blamed for the failure of the siege. His reputation took a blow from which he would never fully recover. It was bad enough that Paris was being blockaded, but then in the autumn of 1432, the plague arrived. Small and large-scale outbreaks of the Black Death were frequent and intermittent throughout the fourteenth and fifteenth centuries, and the one which struck Paris that summer and autumn was no exception. As Bedford limped back to Paris, depressed and with his health failing once again, his was for the second time in his life to be struck with a double tragedy. In November, at the height of the outbreak of the plague, his beloved wife Anne died.

Chapter Twelve

Final Years

Anne of Burgundy was only 28 or 29 years old when she was struck down by the plague in late 1432. She was seriously ill for some time before her death. Her husband made a procession around various churches in Paris on 10 November where prayers and masses were said for her recovery, and she was tended by the best physicians, but nothing could be done. She died on the fourteenth day of the month and was buried on 8 January the following year in the church of the Celestines in Paris, the order to whom she was so devoted. On the day of her funeral, Bedford issued alms, or small gifts of money to some 13,000 people who were present or at least stood in the streets as her cortege passed by.

Later, a story would grow that she had become infected when visiting the sick and bringing food to the poor and plague victims. Such stories were usually designed to emphasise the Christian charity and virtues of the people about whom they were told – but it's not impossible that Anne would have done such a thing. Her nine-year marriage to John had been happy, but childless. Although John had been able to father two illegitimate children in the years before their marriage, children with him Anne might have been close, the couple were for some reason never able to have any children of their own. A chronicler remarked that John suffered 'great sorrow of heart' at his wife's death: probably a classic understatement. As his pilgrimage showed, John would have done almost anything to save her.

John survived the outbreak of plague that claimed the life of his wife; we don't even know if he was ever infected. His family seemed to be great survivors when it came to the disease which killed so many: they were killed by battle, dysentery or the machinations of their political enemies. Ironically, in the month Anne died, a cardinal of the church was trying to broker peace negotiations between France and England which went on for months but ultimately came to nothing. Now that Anne was gone though, the glue which held the alliance of England and Burgundy together began to disintegrate. John knew it. He'd always been a keen observer of events and could see it coming with the truces and negotiations as well as the threats and ultimatums which Burgundy had made against England and with Anne gone there was almost nothing to hold it together except the distant memory of what Charles had done to Phillip's father all those years before and his own determination.

Only a day after his wife's death, John attended a meeting of the Estates of France. Throwing himself into his duties seems to have been John's normal response to grief or extreme stress. Today, he'd probably be called as workaholic, but as he grew older, and his health began to go into decline even John began to realise he was not invincible, and he had to start relying more and more on others. One such person was friend and the chancellor of France, Louis of Luxembourg. Louis' influence was so great that there were whisperings in Paris that he was the one who was truly in charge of the city, rather than Bedford or the distant king of England. In the spring of 1433, Louis introduced John to his beautiful teenage niece, Jacquetta. In March, less than four months after the death of Anne, the 43-year-old John married Jacquetta who was perhaps only 17 or 18 years of age. The marriage was performed by her uncle, and unlike his marriage to Anne, there had been no lengthy betrothal or protracted negotiations. The wedding seems to have been unexpected for everyone. John seems to have believed that it was necessary to form an alliance with the House of Luxembourg, which was beneficial to England, which had probably been his chancellor's plan all along. When Philippe of Burgundy heard what had happened, however, he was furious. Always tetchy about his honour and anything which he perceived as a threat, Phillippe was incensed that John had wed the daughter of one of his vassals without his consent as much as he was insulted at the affront to his sister's memory.

John's second marriage, thus, created a rift between him and the duke of Burgundy which never healed. In the same month of his wedding, when John was attending the peace negotiations with France, he and Burgundy had agreed to a meeting in St Omer, but both requested the other come privately to their lodgings to meet. They did not want to see each other in public, despite Cardinal Beaufort's (who was back in France for the same round of peace negotiations) best attempts to bring about a reconciliation between them. It is unlikely they ever met again, except in a formal capacity and their relationship was never repaired. Phillippe, however, did seem to want to repair his relationship with Charles. There was a six-year truce agreed between him and Charles. They may have come to a more permanent arrangement in 1432–33 if the French had not failed to turn up to the negotiations brokered by one Cardinal Albergati with the intent of ending the war. By the time the French delegation did turn up, the English had begun a new offensive, and it all came to nothing except a four-month truce.

In April 1423 Bedford arranged a joint meeting of the English royal council of Henry VI, and the council which was in Paris which he had presided over many times. He needed the two to co-operate because almost every time he had asked for aid from England, it had been refused, was late, or had failed to materialise altogether. He needed the English council to see firsthand what the situation in France was like, and to knock some of the members heads together if necessary. He arranged the joint meeting to be held in Calais in April. Two months before the meeting took place, the Calais garrison mutinied. Their pay had apparently stopped altogether that year after having been paid only in dribs and drabs in the previous few years. This situation was due largely to the penny-pinching on the part of the English council who liked to redirect money from one place to fund whatever military project was current at the time. In April, John was forced to trick the garrison into submission in order to gain entry to Calais. He gave them documents promising them the money they needed on condition they allowed him free entry, and then entered with his retinue and had them arrested and banished. The conference finally took place in May, and the same month the town of St Valary was taken by the French. In an embarrassing display of the divisions within the English council, Cardinal Beaufort and the archbishop of Canterbury were required to empty their personal coffers and use the money for their expenses to pay for English's ally Jean of Luxembourg to try to protect Burgundian and English territory. Again, an expeditionary force which was supposed to come from England arrived, but it was only half the size it was meant to be, and again the pay for soldiers was not guaranteed with much of the government pleading poverty. Bedford tried to get the council to give him firm promises about what their plans were for the future of the war and France and where the money and soldiers he always needed her going to come from. They could not or would not answer.

Hence, in June 1433, Bedford decided that his only choice was to return to England once again, to explain to the Lords in person that the future of the English kingdom in France was in jeopardy, and all could be lost unless they acted fast. He would be personally present at the Lords for the first time in many years and would once more bring the council and his brother who had been fighting with Cardinal Beaufort for some time to heel. Although both Bedford and Gloucester were now in their forties and Gloucester for his part should certainly have known better, the factionalism caused by personal divisions and animosities were still causing problems at the heart of Henry V's government. Bedford sent out one of his friends to sound out public opinion before returning to England in late June, probably not long before or after his forty-fourth birthday on the twentieth. After an initially frosty reception, the statesman seems to have been well received in his homeland.

Bedford brought his new wife Jacquetta with him, but unlike Anne, Jacquette did not represent the alliance with Burgundy which had been so beneficial and popular. Very few knew about her, and her Uncle Louis was rumoured to by some to be the proxy ruler of France with the ailing duke of Bedford under his control. On 18 July, Bedford addressed the Lords presided over by his 10-year-old nephew and said his piece. Some had dared to suggest that the problems in France were caused by mismanagement and negligence on his own part: this was tantamount to accusing him of treason and was something he would not tolerate. The idea that Bedford had enriched himself at the expense of the territories in France or had ever acted in a treacherous way was laughable. He'd been loyal to a fault for his entire life, often putting his own interests and desires aside to work for the good of the kingdom or for what his family members wanted. Bedford was angry and wasn't willing to accept any of the government's excuses or evasions that sitting. As one of the senior nobles of the realm, he took virtual control of the council again, for the second time in ten years. He set about replacing some of his brother's favourites with his own men once again and by 24 November (the Lords had to be prorogued for several months because of an outbreak of plague) the Lords were begging Bedford to return home and remain in England for the rest of his life. There probably weren't many present that session who remembered the years in which Bedford had run the country as Lieutenant during Henry V's absence. Yet to them he had come to represent everything which Beaufort and Gloucester did not: stability, unity, an unshakable commitment to duty and putting the good of the country above personal vendettas and self-interest.

Bedford was simply more used to running a country or a duchy than most of his peers – and better at doing so. The Lords and the people of England had come to see Bedford as a saviour and a solution to the division among the nobles who surrounded the king for so long. They spoke of him as an exemplar of good rule who upheld the king's laws and peace with an even hand. Perhaps England could, indeed, have benefitted from having Bedford at the helm as he had been fifteen years earlier. Perhaps Bedford himself even yearned to return home permanently. He even purchased a Penshurst House in Kent and the estate that went with it to use as a sort of retirement home. Bedford stayed in England for fifteen months, once again seeing to business and spending some time overseeing the government of the realm. In June 1434, he made an impassioned plea to the council to continue the war effort and pursue it with as much vigour as they once had. All had gone well in France, John said until the siege of Orléans, which he considered the turning point. Now the people of Normandy who were subjects of King Henry were in dire straits and 'hath been driven to the extreme of poverty'. He also reminded them of how many English lives had been lost over the years. It did very little good, for in the end, Bedford was one of the only men who still truly believed in the continuation of the English kingdom of France. Promises were, of course, made, money was pledged and so were soldiers but very little was done, and in the end, it was the France who called for John to return because once again anarchy was on the rise and brigands roamed the countryside. Paris was once more threatened. As he had been for so many years John was being pulled in two directions. The government of England could not or would not function without him and fell to infighting, but it also seemed that every time he left France, chaos ensued.

On 30 August 1434, as a gesture of kindness to his uncle, Henry VI legitimised Bedford's bastard son, Richard. Such an act was performed by either an act of the Lords or a declaration of the king, and a copy of the declaration was apparently sent to Rouen. Decades earlier, Richard II had legitimised the Beauforts: the bastard children of John of Gaunt, but with them there was one key difference: Gaunt had married their mother, Katherine Swynford. The legitimisation of John's son would allow him to inherit some of his father's property although he would still not be able to succeed to the title of Duke of Bedford nor would he be in the line of succession. Richard was by this time probably in his late teens and may have married shortly after his legitimisation. His wife was named Isabel. Her origins are as obscure as Richard's but she seems to have been a woman of the gentry classes who had already been twice widowed. As much as the legitimisation of his son might have been a comfort to John, it also comes with a note of sadness because it was an admission that John had basically given up hope of ever having another child with his wife. Although he had only been married to Jacquetta for a year and seems to have wed her in the vague hope of an heir as well as for the alliance with her uncle, he may have taken a step back and began looking at things more realistically by 1434. John's increasingly common bouts of ill-health may have convinced John had he did not have long left for the world and there is an underlying tone of weariness in a lot of his late correspondence as well as his discussions with Henry VI. It was at the council in 1434 that he spoke of the people of England being punished for their failure to trust in God by the loss of their territory, disease, poverty and humiliation by Joan of Arc. His speech to the council, which was to be his last, reveals that John had always believed his brother's mission was divinely ordained as was his nephew's rule in France. It had always been about more than just fulfilling his brother's deathbed wish to John. He saw himself as continuing the work his brother had left undone – to reclaim and secure the rule of the territories in France England had once owned with the help of God.

John finally returned to France in August 1434. When he stepped aboard his ship, it was to be the last time he ever saw England. He arrived just before another major revolt against English rule, this time by the peasants. It all began with a series of harsh winters and crop failures which led to poverty and hardship in Normandy and throughout Europe, which was exacerbated by an outbreak of plague: the same one which had killed Anne of Burgundy. The men of some English garrisons did not help with they pillaged food in the countryside, often because they pillaged food and supplies from the neighbouring countryside: in reaction the peasanty rebelled and killed a number of English people. In reprisal, a former English soldier named Richard Venables who had become a freebooter and bandit took a company of men and slaughtered 1,200 French villagers. Venables had been in France for a few years and had served in a garrison in the service of Bedford before going rogue. It was a story which was all too common in Normandy. The English authorities in Normandy responded swiftly: several of Venables men were rounded up an executed on the orders of Sir John Fastolf. Venables, though, escaped, so Bedford put a price on his head and when the man was apprehended John brought the full force of the law down upon him. He had Venables hanged, drawn and quartered. Bedford could be implacable to people he considered to have betrayed him, but his willingness to make an example of a man who had cut down so many innocent Norman villagers shows he was committed to impartiality in justice. Most would not have taken such action against one of their own countrymen, but Bedford understood the necessity of such gestures. It was though a case of too little, too late. The people of Normandy took the massacre and the presence of other bandits like Venables as a sign the English could no longer protect them.

A month before, thousands of Norman villagers and some gentry had risen in revolt and sent to Charles of France for assistance. Despite Bedford's best efforts to assert justice, English morale was failing. The English no longer trusted the Normans among whom they had lived for so long, and soldiers began to desert in large numbers from towns and sites which they had been besieging for months or even years. Building work on a grand royal palace which had been designed by Henry V began, but the place was constructed as a fortress rather than as the pleasure palace Henry had envisioned. The English nobility was taking refuge behind walls and effectively hiding from their own Norman subjects and compatriots, and new laws were passed to ensure fewer Frenchmen were included in armies and garrisons. No longer were the English to be the colonizers who lived among the Normans and fought alongside Burgundians as allies. Under the new generation of commanders in the mid-1430s, they degenerated into an occupying force.

In December 1434, John returned to Paris to a lukewarm welcome, and to a city much reduced by poverty, blockade, war and famine. He was no longer welcomed as a hero or great ruler as he had been in the past, and indeed was hardly welcomed at all. The people of Paris seem to have blamed him for the failure of the peace negotiations in 1432–33 and for abandoning him during a time of such turmoil. Two months later, by which time Louis of Luxembourg had stepped down from his position as chancellor, John of Bedford also departed the city for the last time. He had decided to move back to Rouen. Unlike the last time though, he did not have his beloved Anne beside him, nor were the English firmly in charge of Normandy or the capital of France.

Congress of Arras

In June, the earl of Arundel died because of infection from an injury he'd sustained trying to regain yet another French town which had been taken. John had sent him on the expedition and probably now blamed himself for the death of another English commander as well as several hundred of his men. In May 1435 that the English heard peace negotiations were being held near Arras, in the region of Artois in Burgundy, but it wasn't until July that the English delegation arrived. Arras was not like other peace conferences or negotiations before it. Now that Anne of Burgundy was dead there was little still connecting Phillip the Good to England except for the oaths he had once made. Charles VII's delegation were willing to make significant territorial concessions to England but the lands they offered were to be held 'in French sovereignty' which meant the king of England was to do homage to the French king for them, and the Lancastrian claim was not to be recognised. It is likely these offers were only made to win over Phillip of Burgundy and make the English appear unreasonable for not accepting them, because acknowledging Henry VI's claim was not something they were willing to compromise on.

Wranglings and negotiations continued for a few months. Eventually the French offered that Henry VI could have all of Normandy, but he would still have been required to swear fealty to the king of France. However, they were willing to delay that for seven years until he had come of age. The English, of course, did not accept as this situation would have put them right back to where the English kings in the fourteenth century had been, and negated almost everything Henry V and so many of his nobles had fought for. More, the English were being treated as though they had basically lost the war in France, which had not happened.

On 6 September, the English delegation departed from Arras because they had reached an impasse. The duke of Burgundy was furious and warned them that he would make a separate peace with Charles. He carried out his promise exactly two weeks later. On 28 September, Cardinal Albergati and a French compatriot proclaimed that the Treaty of Troyes was null and void, as was Phillip's oath to uphold it. The following day, a formal treaty was made between Phillip and Charles was made and proclaimed to a packed congregation in the cathedral church of St Vaast in Arras. John had not attended any part of the Congress of Arras.

On 14 September, eight days after the departure of the English delegation and a week before the treaty of Arras was sealed, John of Bedford died in his house in Rouen. He was 46 years old and was surrounded by both of his children, Richard and Marie. John would probably have been glad he didn't live to hear about Phillip abandoning the Anglo-Burgundian alliance, but he no doubt guessed that it was coming. In the end, it was the sickness which had beset him for several years which appears to have claimed his life. Yet he may have also despaired of seeing his one-time brother-in-law abandoning everything he had fought and stood for, and the future of English rule in France teetering on the edge of a knife. Perhaps in the end, John just gave up.

Mary, his daughter, had recently become betrothed to a French nobleman named Pierre de Montferrand; he was a loyal partisan of the English and probably came from Gascony in Southern France. Montferrand fought loyally for England and Henry VI for many years after their marriage. Although he swore an oath to Charles VII after England's final defeat in 1453, he never broke faith with Henry VI and was ultimately exiled from France. He was executed in 1454 after having been caught in France in breach of his sentence of exile. The last known record of Mary comes the 1460s, nearly thirty years after John's death, when she was granted a pension by none other than Edward IV. When her husband was executed, her children (and John's grandchildren) remained in France as hostages whilst Mary was forced to return to the country, she had not called home for more than two decades: not since her father had sailed to England for the last time in 1433. It is possible to trace John's descendants through Mary for several generations as the Montferrand family remained prominent in France. It is ironic that the descendants of John, Duke of Bedford survived among the French gentry and nobility and never again had any connection with England. One wonders if they even knew about their ancestor of if this was considered a shameful family connection which was not talked about.

Her brother, Richard inherited the castle and surrounding lands of La Haye-du-Puits in France. No record of Richard survives into the reign of the Yorkist kings: he may have felt the need to keep his head down because he was not only John's male heir, but he had also been legitimised and so could have bene perceived as a threat. Or he may simply have died before the deposition of Henry VI.

John made a will a few days before his death in which he said he wanted to be buried in Rouen Cathedral. His wish was granted. Originally, his grave was marked with a grand black marble tomb and a plaque emblazoned with his coat of arms and that of the order of the Garter. His tomb survived until 1562 when Rouen Cathedral was sacked by French Huguenots, and all trace was finally removed during the political turmoil of the eighteenth-century revolution. Today, all that remains is a slab of stone near the left side of what would have been the high altar. His death really represented the end of an era. Although the English held on in France for some eighteen years after his death and were not finally expelled until 1453, John of Bedford was England's 'only statesman who understood the challenges of the dual monarchy, or by the end truly believed in it'.[1] Humphrey, Duke of Gloucester complained loudly about England not being committed enough to the war in France in the 1440s, but he never really did anything and never went to France. He was committed more to the idea of the dual monarchy in theory than in practice, like his brother had been.

John, Duke of Bedford might also be considered the last member of the Lancastrian royal family who was a genuinely great ruler. He ruled England in all but name for four years and Normandy for the best part of thirteen. Apart from the inevitable grievances about taxation to fund military expeditions, few seem to have had any real objections to John's rule. Indeed, John was more likely to be criticised for his equitable view of justice which meant that he did not show undue favour to anyone when it came to law and order. He would not spare the guilty because they were English or punish people more harshly because they were French, as many of his contemporaries would have done.

The periods in which he held power in France and England were notable free of the divisions and violent factionalism which poisoned English politics in the later part of the fifteenth century. On the two occasions in which John had returned to England after becoming regent of France he did his best to fix the divisions and deal with corruption. After his death, people looked back with nostalgia on the life and career of John. He wasn't known, like his brother as 'good Duke Humphrey', but perhaps he should have been.

Acknowledgements

Many were involved in helping this book to come into being. First, I'd like to extend my thanks to Sarah-Beth Watkins at Pen and Sword for allowing me an extension to my deadline.

At the time, I didn't know how much I'd need it, what with battling Covid and changing jobs. Also, thanks to Tara McEvoy of Faber books for sending me a review copy the fifth and last title in Johnathan Sumption's Hundred Years War series just before the release date. The book was so much help.

Special thanks to my mother and proofreader – for the encouragement and, of course, proofreading this book.

Finally, to everyone on all my research trips who was patient enough to listen to me enthuse about John, Duke of Bedford, Henry V, Margaret of Anjou, and other fifteenth-century figures. If nobody was interested, I don't know if I could have done this. Special thanks to the good people of Rouen who didn't mind this crazy English woman coming to see the sites in your beautiful city even when they found out who I was writing about.

Notes

Chapter One

1. E. Carleton Williams, *My Lord of Bedford, 1389–1435* (Longmans, 1963), p. 2.
2. Ibid.
3. Bagpipes or proto bagpipes were not an instrument purely associated with Scotland at this time but were popular and played throughout Europe and other parts of the world. See Malcolm Vale, *Henry V: The Conscience of a King* (Yale University Press, 2016), pp. 218-19.
4. See David Baldwin, *The Kingmaker's Sisters: Six Powerful Women of the Wars of the Roses* (The History Press, 2023), pp. 30-31.
5. Kathryn Warner, *Blood Roses: The Houses of Lancaster and York before the Wars of the Roses* (The History Press, 2018), p. 262.
6. Ibid.
7. Jeanne E. Krochalis, 'The Books and Reading of Henry V and His Circle', *The Chaucer Review*, vol. 23, no. 1 (1988), p. 51.
8. Chris Given-Wilson, *Henry IV* (Yale University Press, 2016), pp. 66-69.
9. Ibid, p. 72.
10. Ibid, p. 74. Lionel of Antwerp was taken ill and died shortly after his marriage to Violante, and there has been speculation over the years that he was in fact poisoned by his new father-in-law Gian Visconti the father of Violante and Gian Galeazzo, visconti. This might have made Henry's meeting with his son rather awkward.
11. Ian Mortimer, *The Fears of Henry IV: The Life of England's Self-Made King* (Vintage, 2008), p. 128.

12. Alison Weir and others speculate that Queen Anne may have actually died as early as the third of June, one day before Mary de Bohun. Alison Weir, *Queens of the Age of Chivalry* (Jonathan Cape, 2022), p. 382.
13. Sheen Palace was located in modern Richmond on Thames, and the later Richmond Palace was built on the same site.
14. Kathryn Warner, *Richard II: A True King's Fall* (The History Press, 2019), pp. 196-99.

Chapter Two

1. Ibid, pp. 242-43.
2. Michael Bennett, *Richard II and the Revolution of 1399* (Sutton, 2006), pp. 132-33.
3. Jean Froissart, *Chronicles*, trans. Geoffrey Brereton (Penguin, 1978), p437.
4. Ibid.
5. Given-Wilson, *Henry IV*, p. 116.
6. Warner, *Richard II*, p. 258.
7. Kathryn Warner, *John of Gaunt: Son of One King, Father of Another* (Amberley, 2022), p. 253.
8. Bennett, *Richard II and the Revolution*, p. 149.
9. Ibid, p. 168.
10. *Chronicque de la Traison et Mort de Richart Deux Roy Dengleterre*, ed. Benjamin Williams (London, 1846), pp. 220-21.

Chapter Three

1. This was Edward of Norwich the eldest son of Edmund of Langley, duke of York, and another first cousin of Henry IV.
2. *Chronicque de la Traison et Mort*, pp. 249-50.
3. Given-Wilson, *Henry IV*, p. 220.

4. Given-Wilson, *Henry IV*, p. 220.

5. Ibid, pp. 226-27.

6. Ibid.

7. S.J. Lang, 'The Philomena of John Bradmore and its Middle English Derivative: A Perspective on Surgery in Late Medieval England', University of St Andrews unpublished Ph.D. thesis, 1998, pp. 65-66

8. Juliet Barker, *Agincourt: The King, the Campaign, the Battle* (Little Brown, 2005), pp. 52-53.

9. This was the Ralph Neville who was the grandfather of the famous Richard Neville, Earl of Warwick 'the Kingmaker'. He was also grandfather to the Yorkist kings through his daughter by Joan Beaufort, Cecily Neville.

10. Given-Wilson, *Henry IV*, p. 266.

11. Ibid, 267.

12. Mortimer, *Fears of Henry IV*, p. 293.

13. *Royal and Historical Letters during the Reign of Henry the Fourth*, ed. F. Hingeston, vol. 2 (London, 1860), pp. 61-63.

14. Given-Wilson, *Henry IV*, pp. 267-68.

15. Mortimer, Op Cit, p. 294-95.

16. Given-Wilson, *Henry IV*, p. 269.

17. Mortimer, *Fears of Henry IV*, p. 296.

18. *Royal and Historical Letters*, pp. 228-31.

19. Ibid, pp. 219-24.

20. Ibid, pp. xv, 73.

21. Given-Wilson, *Henry IV*, p. 307. See also *Chronicle of London from 1089 to 1483*, ed. N. Nicholas and E. Tyrell (London, 1827), p. 93. Eastcheap was part of the area of London devoted to markets at this time. Eastcheap was specifically home to fish markets. Possibly the retainers were there to obtain supplies since fish were an important part of the medieval diet, or had accommodation nearby. Eastcheap was also the location of the fictional tavern frequented by John Falstaff and his band of ne'er do wells in Shakespeare's *Henry V*.

22. 'Leprosy' seems to have been used as a generic term for any kind of severe skin condition in the medieval period rather than the specific condition known as Hansen's Disease today.

Chapter Four

1. 'Henry V: April 1414.' *Parliament Rolls of Medieval England,* eds. Chris Given-Wilson, Paul Brand, Seymour Phillips, Mark Ormrod, Geoffrey Martin, Anne Curry, and Rosemary Horrox (Boydell, 2005). *British History Online.* http://www.british-history.ac.uk/no-series/parliament-rolls-medieval/april-1414, accessed 3 August 2023,

2. It has also been proposed that York's poem might not have been written with a romantic intent, and that he was commissioned to write it by Henry as a celebration of his marriage. This is possible as well. See Krochalis, *The Books and Reading of Henry V and His Circle,* p. 55.

3. Margaret Holland was not simply Thomas' aunt by marriage, she was also the first cousin of his mother, Mary de Bohun. In addition to that, her brother and uncle were executed for their involvement in the Epiphany Rising against Henry IV.

4. Thomson, John A. F., 'Oldcastle, John, Baron Cobham (d. 1417), soldier, heretic, and rebel', *Oxford Dictionary of National Biography.* https://www.oxforddnb.com/view/10.1093/ref:odnb/9780198614128.001.0001/odnb-9780198614128-e-20674, accessed 4 August 2023.

5. Teresa Cole, *Henry V: The Life of the Warrior King and the Battle of Agincourt* (Amberley, 2015), p. 75.

6. John Goodall, *The Castle: A History* (Yale University Press, 2022), pp. 164-65.

7. Ibid.

8. Michael Brown, *A Guide to Medieval Gardens: Gardens in the Age of Chivalry* (Pen & Sword, 2022), p. 17.

9. Given-Wilson, *Henry IV*, pp. 265-66.
10. Vale, *Conscience of the King*, p. 218.

Chapter Five

1. 'Close Rolls, Henry V: August 1415,' in *Calendar of Close Rolls, Henry V: Volume 1, 1413–1419*, ed. A.E. Stamp (London: His Majesty's Stationery Office, 1929), 231. *British History Online*, http://www.british-history.ac.uk/cal-close-rolls/hen5/vol1/p.231a, accessed August 24, 2023.
2. 'Close Rolls, Henry V: October 1415', pp. 231-34. *British History Online*, http://www.british-history.ac.uk/cal-close-rolls/hen5/vol1/pp. 231-234, accessed August 24, 2023.
3. 'Close Rolls, Henry V: November 1415', pp. 234-36. *British History Online*, http://www.british-history.ac.uk/cal-close-rolls/hen5/vol1/pp. 234-36, accessed August 24, 2023.
4. Barker, *Agincourt*, p. 350.
5. Vale, *Conscience of the King*, pp. 214-16.
6. Sigismund became a close friend of Henry. He was also, ironically, the brother of Anne of Bohemia who had been marred to Richard II.
7. Jonathan Sumption, *Cursed Kings: Hundred Years War, Vol IV* (Faber, 2015), pp. 497-98.
8. Richard Wadge, *The Battle of Verneuil 1424: A Second Agincourt* (Cheltenham, 2015), p. 114.
9. Sumption, *Cursed Kings*, p. 747. Kindle Edition.
10. Williams, *My Lord of Bedford*, p. 44.
11. Vale, *Conscience of the King*, p. 51.
12. Stratford, J., 'John [John of Lancaster], Duke of Bedford (1389–1435), regent of France and prince', *Oxford Dictionary of National Biography*. https://www.oxforddnb.com/view/10.1093/ref:odnb/9780198614128.001.0001/odnb-9780198614128-e-14844, accessed 24 October 2023.

13. Williams, *My Lord of Bedford*, pp. 46-47. Williams suggests that it was Joanna's reputation for eccentricity and her rumoured sexual promiscuity which made John reluctant to take up her offer, but it was more likely to have been the practicalities of the war in France as well as his commitments in England whilst it was going on.

14. Ibid, pp. 47-48.

15. Ibid, pp. 41-42.

16. Jones, M., 'Joan [Joan of Navarre] (1368–1437), queen of England, second consort of Henry IV', *Oxford Dictionary of National Biography*. https://www.oxforddnb.com/view/10.1093/ref:odnb/9780198614128.001.0001/odnb-9780198614128-e-14824, accessed 22 October 2023.

17. Bart van Loo and Nancy Forest-Flier, trans., *The Burgundians: A Vanished Empire* (London, 2021), p. 268.

18. Juliet Barker, *Conquest: The English Kingdom of France, 1417–1450* (Little Brown, 2010), pp. 26-27.

19. The account in Bart van Loo's book says Burgundy was struck between the shoulder blades before another can and struck him in the head and someone else finished him off when he was down, pp. 269-70. Juliet Barker instead reports that he was struck in the face and reports the words of du Châtel as 'it is time'.

20. 'Henry V: October 1419', *Parliament Rolls of Medieval England*, eds. Chris Given-Wilson, Paul Brand, Seymour Phillips, Mark Ormrod, Geoffrey Martin, Anne Curry, and Rosemary Horrox (Boydell, 2005). *British History Online*, http://www.british-history.ac.uk/no-series/parliament-rolls-medieval/october-1419, accessed 17 September 2023.

21. Wadge, *Battle of Verneuil*, p. 134.

Chapter Six

1. Christopher Allmand, *Lancastrian Normandy, 1415–1450: The History of a Medieval Occupation* (Oxford, 1983), p. 21.

2. Wadge, *Battle of Verneuil*, p. 134.
3. Sumption, *Cursed Kings*, p. 1020. Kindle Edition.
4. Williams, *My Lord of Bedford*, p. 62.
5. Ibid, p. 70.
6. Vale, Henry V, pp. 170-71.
7. Sumption, *Cursed Kings*, p. 1149, Kindle Edition.
8. Nathen Amin, *The House of Beaufort: The Bastard Line Which Captured the Crown* (Amberley, 2017), p. 164.
9. Ibid, p. 1155.

Chapter Seven

1. Jonathan Sumption, *The Hundred Years War V: Triumph and Illusion* (Faber, 2023), p. 4.
2. Ibid.
3. Ibid, p. 61.
4. Richard Ballard, *England, France and Aquitaine: From Victory to Defeat in the Hundred Years War* (Pen and Sword, 2020), p. 33.
5. Richard Vaughan, *Phillip the Good: The Apogee of Burgundy* (Boydell, 2004), p. 9.
6. Ballard, *England, France and Aquitaine*, p. 32. See also, Allmand, *Lancastrian Normandy*, p. 21.
7. Sumption, *Triumph and Illusion*, p. 151.
8. Ibid, p. 150.
9. Ibid, pp. 95-96.
10. Wadge, *Battle of Verneuil*, pp. 82-83.
11. Vaughan, *Phillip the Good*, p. 15.
12. Ibid.
13. Sumption, *Triumph and Illusion*, pp. 96-97.
14. Ibid.
15. Wadge, *Battle of Verneuil*, p. 180.

Chapter Eight

1. Ibid, p. 221.
2. Sumption, *Triumph and Illusion*, pp. 141-42.

Chapter Nine

1. Allmand, *Lancastrian Normandy*, pp. 252-53.
2. Ibid, p. 191.

Chapter Ten

1. Helen Castor, *Joan of Arc: A History* (Faber, 2015), p. 100.
2. Yolande of Aragon was also the grandmother of Margaret of Anjou, who would go on to marry King Henry VI of England.
3. Barker, *Conquest*, p. 112.
4. Ibid, pp. 121-22.
5. Williams, p. 171.
6. Ibid, p. 172.
7. Castor, *Joan of Arc*, p. 141.
8. Sumption, *Triumph and Illusion*, p. 347.

Chapter Eleven

1. Sumption, *Triumph and Illusion*, p. 339-40.
2. Allmand, *Lancastrian Normandy*, p. 26.
3. Barker, *Conquest*, pp. 178-79.
4. Castor, *Joan of Arc*, p. 191.
5. Sumption, *Triumph and Illusion*, p. 401.

Chapter Twelve

1. Ibid, p. 478.

Bibliography

Primary Sources

Chronicque de la Traison et Mort de Richart Deux Roy Dengleterre.
Ed. Benjamin Williams (London, 1846).

Froissart, Jean. *Chronicles*. Trans. Geoffrey Brereton (London: Penguin, 1978).

Henry V: April 1414. *Parliament Rolls of Medieval England*. Eds. Chris Given-Wilson, Paul Brand, Seymour Phillips, Mark Ormrod, Geoffrey Martin, Anne Curry, and Rosemary Horrox (Woodbridge: Boydell, 2005). *British History Online*.

Henry V: October 1419. *Parliament Rolls of Medieval England*. Eds. Chris Given-Wilson, Paul Brand, Seymour Phillips, Mark Ormrod, Geoffrey Martin, Anne Curry, and Rosemary Horrox (Woodbridge: Boydell, 2005). *British History Online*.

Hingeston, F., ed. *Royal and Historical Letters during the Reign of Henry the Fourth*, vol. 2 (London, 1860).

Stamp, A.E., ed. 'Close Rolls, Henry V: August 1415.' *Calendar of Close Rolls, Henry V: Volume 1, 1413–1419* (London: His Majesty's Stationery Office, 1929). *British History Online*.

Secondary Sources

Allmand, Christopher. *Henry V: Yale English Monarchs Series* (London: Yale University Press, 1997).

Allmand, Christopher. *Lancastrian Normandy, 1415–1450* (Oxford University Press, 1983).

Amin, Nathen. *The House of Beaufort: The Bastard Line that Captured the Crown* (Stroud: Amberley, 2017).

Barker, Juliett. *Agincourt: The King, the Campaign, the Battle* (London: Little Brown, 2006).

Barker, Juliett. *Conquest: The English Kingdom of France, 1417–1450.* (London: Little Brown, 2010).

Ballard, Richard. *England, France and Aquitaine: From Victory to Defeat in the Hundred Years War* (Barnsley: Pen and Sword, 2020).

Brown, Michael. *A Guide to Medieval Gardens: Gardens in the Age of Chivalry* (Barnsley: Pen and Sword, 2022).

Bennett, Michael. *Richard II and the Revolution of 1399* (Stroud: Sutton, 2006).

Castor, Helen. *Joan of Arc: A History* (Faber: London, 2015).

Cole, Teresa. *Henry V: The Life of the Warrior King and the Battle of Agincourt* (Stroud: Amberley 2016).

Goodall, John. *The Castle: A History* (London: Yale University Press, 2022).

Given-Wilson, Chris. *Henry IV* (New Haven: Yale University Press, 2016).

Jones, M. 'Joan [Joan of Navarre] (1368–1437), queen of England, second consort of Henry IV'. *Oxford Dictionary of National Biography* (Oxford: Oxford University Press, 2014).

Krochalis, Jeanne E. 'The Books and Reading of Henry V and His Circle.' *The Chaucer Review*, vol. 23, no. 1 (1988): pp 50-77.

Lang, S.J. 'The Philomena of John Bradmore and its Middle English Derivative: A Perspective on Surgery in Late Medieval England'. University of St Andrews unpublished Ph.D. Thesis (1998).

Mortimer, Ian. *The Fears of Henry IV: The Life of England's Self-made King* (London: Vintage, 2008).

Stratford, J. 'John [John of Lancaster], duke of Bedford (1389–1435), regent of France and prince'. *Oxford Dictionary of National Biography* (Oxford: Oxford University Press, 2011).

Sumption, Jonathan. *The Hundred Years War: Vol IV Cursed Kings* (Faber: London, 2015).

Sumption, Jonathan. *The Hundred Years War: Vol V Triumph and Illusion* (Faber: London, 2023).

Thomson, John A.F. 'Oldcastle, John, Baron Cobham (d. 1417), soldier, heretic, and rebel'. *Oxford Dictionary of National Biography* (Oxford: Oxford University Press, 2008).

Vale, Malcolm. *Henry V: Conscience of a King* (London: Yale University Press, 2016).

Van Loo, Bart, and Nancy Forest-Flier, trans. *The Burgundians: A Vanished Empire* (London: Head of Zeus, 2021).

Vaughan, Richard. *Philip the Good: The Apogee of Burgundy* (Woodbridge: Boydell, 2004).

Wadge, Richard. *The Battle of Verneuil 1424: A Second Agincourt* (Stroud: The History Press, 2015).

Warner, K. *John of Gaunt, Son of One King, Father of Another* (Stroud: Amberley, 2022).

Warner, K. *Richard II: A True King's Fall* (Stroud: Amberley, 2019)

Warner, K. *Blood Roses: The Houses of Lancaster and York before the Wars of the Roses* (Stroud: The History Press, 2018).

Weir, Alison. *Queens of the Age of Chivalry* (London: Jonathan Cape, 2022).

Williams, E. Carleton. *My Lord of Bedford, 1389–1435* (London: Longmans, 1963).